bent street 2

Australian LGBTIQA+ arts, writing & ideas

Bent Street is published annually by Clouds of Magellan Press, Melbourne, www.cloudsofmagellanpress.net.

email: cloudsofmagellanpress@gmail.com

Bent Street welcomes contributions and publishes ongoing throughout the year—visit bentstreet.net.

ISBN: (paperback) 978-0-6484604-0-4
ISBN: (ebook) 978-0-6484604-1-1

Editor: Tiffany Jones
Contributing editors: Ashley Sievwright, Gordon Thompson
Logo: Andrew Liu
Design: Gordon Thompson

Cover image: Jamie James | Queerdom

CONTENTS

ANTICIPATION

PEOPLE

ESSAYS, TALKS, POSTS

POETRY

FICTION

ACKNOWLEDGEMENTS

Adam Jones, 'Decaying photo of Freddie Mercury outside Mercury House, Stone Town, Zanzibar, Tanzania' is sourced from Wikimedia.

David Wojnarowicz, 'Untitled (Face in Dirt) 1990-1993' is reproduced courtesy of the Estate of David Wojnarowicz and P.P.O.W, New York—www.ppowgallery.com.

Dennis Altman's article was originally published by the Australian Institute of International Affairs (http://www.internationalaffairs.org.au/australianoutlook/a-locked-closet-lgbti-rights/) 26 Apr 2018.

Maria Palotta-Chiarolli's Executive Summary to *Safe spaces: a new report on LGBTIQA+ Muslims* is reprinted here with kind permission of the author, and Reem Sweid and Zahirah Johari (Research Development and Management, Muslim Collective).

Alison Thorne's *Remembering the Pink Triangle* was originally presented on 30 October 2018 at an event hosted by Rainbow Atheists.

The excerpt from 'Hyperreality' by Lian Low, appears in *Living and Loving in Diversity : an anthology of Australian multicultural queer adventures*, AGMC, (2018), Wakefield Press. Reprinted with kind permission of the Australian LQBTIQ Multicultural Council (AGMC).

The excerpt from *Dear Rachel Maddow* is provided by kind permission of the author, Adrienne Kisner. Copyright © 2018 Adrienne Kisner, per Feiwel and Friends. The novel (ISBN: 125014602X; ISBN13: 9781250146021) was published 5 June 2018 by Feiwel & Friends and is available through Macmillan in the US and online via Amazon and a variety of other outlets.

Senator Janet Rice's Facebook post is reprinted with kind permission of Senator Rice.

Senator Dean Smith's *Together: a senator's perspective* is reprinted with kind permission of Senator Smith and first appeared in Pride WA's 2018 Program.

INTRODUCTION

Welcome back to *Bent Street*, the road less travelled. This year we invited back many well-established citizens from our first *Bent Street* neighbourhood, who share their latest creative works, manifestos, stories, research and essays. However we also opened up the street to a larger party and invited new neighbours over. They include photographers, mixed medium artists, online poets, hypertext manipulators, Twitter-tweeters, young adult novel writers and people working in a range of modern mediums.

Bent Street 2 continues its focus on being an 'annual' publication: featuring works that emerged from LGBTIQA+ and allied creators in 2018, that were on themes arising from 2018, or that reflected back from 2018 to relevant histories. Though the dust finally settled on several nations' marriage rights debates in 2017 (including for Australia), it had no time to collect on other issues. This year we saw an increase in the extreme efforts to silence LGBTIQA+ communities and extreme efforts to uplift them. Australia's Morrison Administration and the sledgehammer of Murdoch Media targeted so-called 'gender whisperers' in Australian schools; whilst both houses of the Australian Parliament debated how best to remove exemptions allowing religious schools to expel and fire LGBT people. The USA's Trump administration actively sought to erase transgender and gender diverse people; whilst activist organisations successfully pressured Twitter to ban misgendering and deadnaming. Some countries opened their doors more widely to LGBTIQA+ asylum seekers; Uganda received at least one notable ex-patriot back showing the complexities of asylum and identity itself.

As the world faced increased normalising pressure from the alt right and gender hegemony traditionalists, 2018 became a year for heroic refusals. This was the year where singer Hayley Kiyoko refused victimisation by calling for a #20gayteen of queer teen love, Olympians refused to be photographed next to politicians who preached hate against them and comic Hannah Gadsby refused to let the world simply laugh at homophobia by calling for more subversive comedy.

Under pressure, we looked to specific heroes for inspiration. Many *Bent Street* contributors recall how they reconnected to heroes who brazenly withstood normalising pressures recently and in the past: Steve RE Pereira recalls his connection to musician Freddie Mercury; Jamie James and Quinn Eades recall their connection to queer performance innovators; Brigitte Lewis recalls her connection to dubious gurus; Guy James Whitworth recalls his connection to Australian gay activist Peter De Waal and Adrienne Kisner recalls her connection to news analyst Rachel Maddow. Other *Bent Street* contributors call for readers to engage in direct acts of subversion: Madison Griffiths offers poetic practice at saying 'no'; Craig Middleton and Nikki Sullivan offer their KINQ Manifesto for queering knowledge industries; Dennis Altman offers hope in redirecting our attention to international developments.

Whilst *Bent Street 2* continues its previous road; we hope its new curves and kinks are enjoyable.

Tiffany Jones—Editor
December 2018

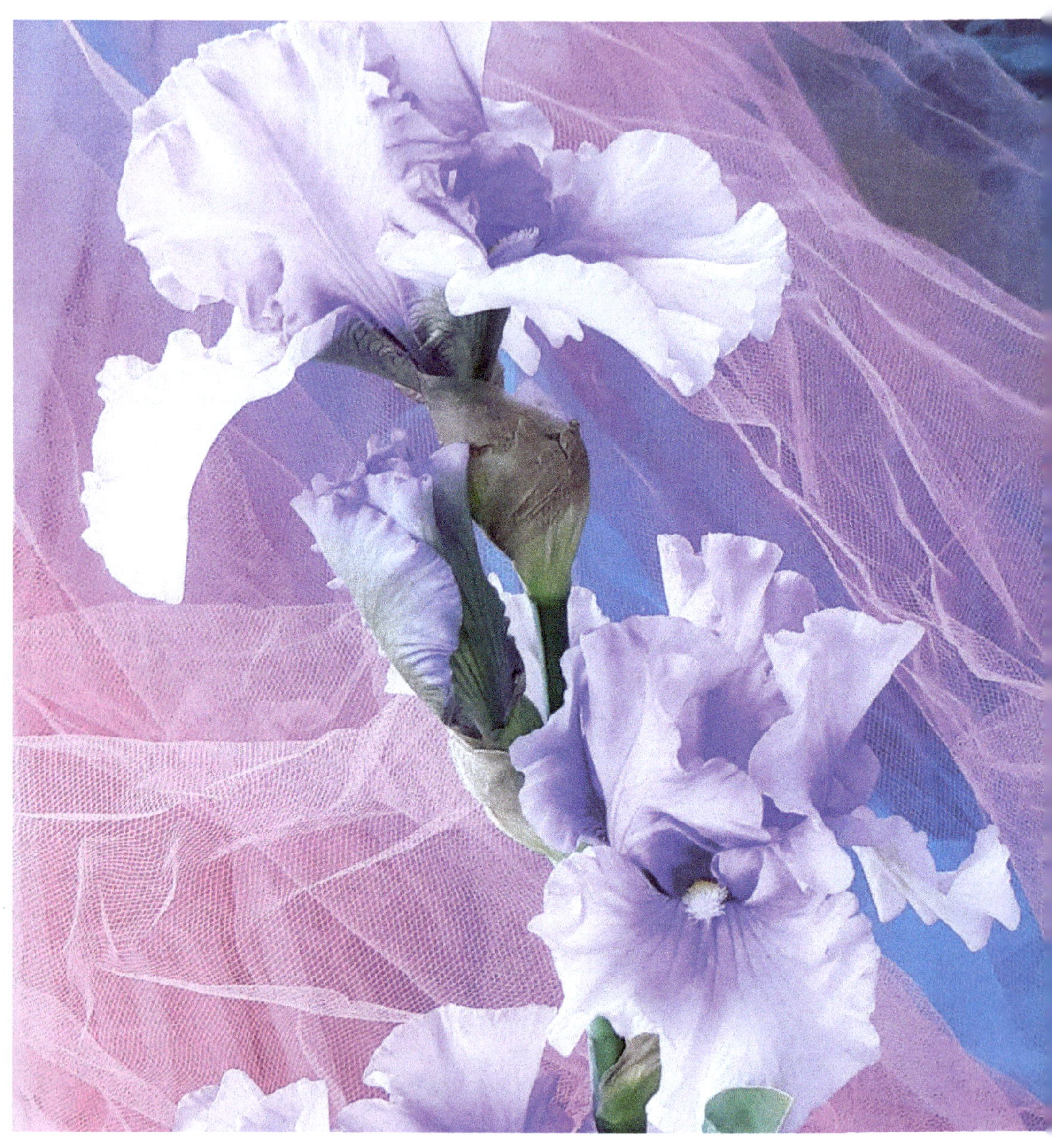

HENRY VON DOUSSA | IRIS 1

PEOPLE

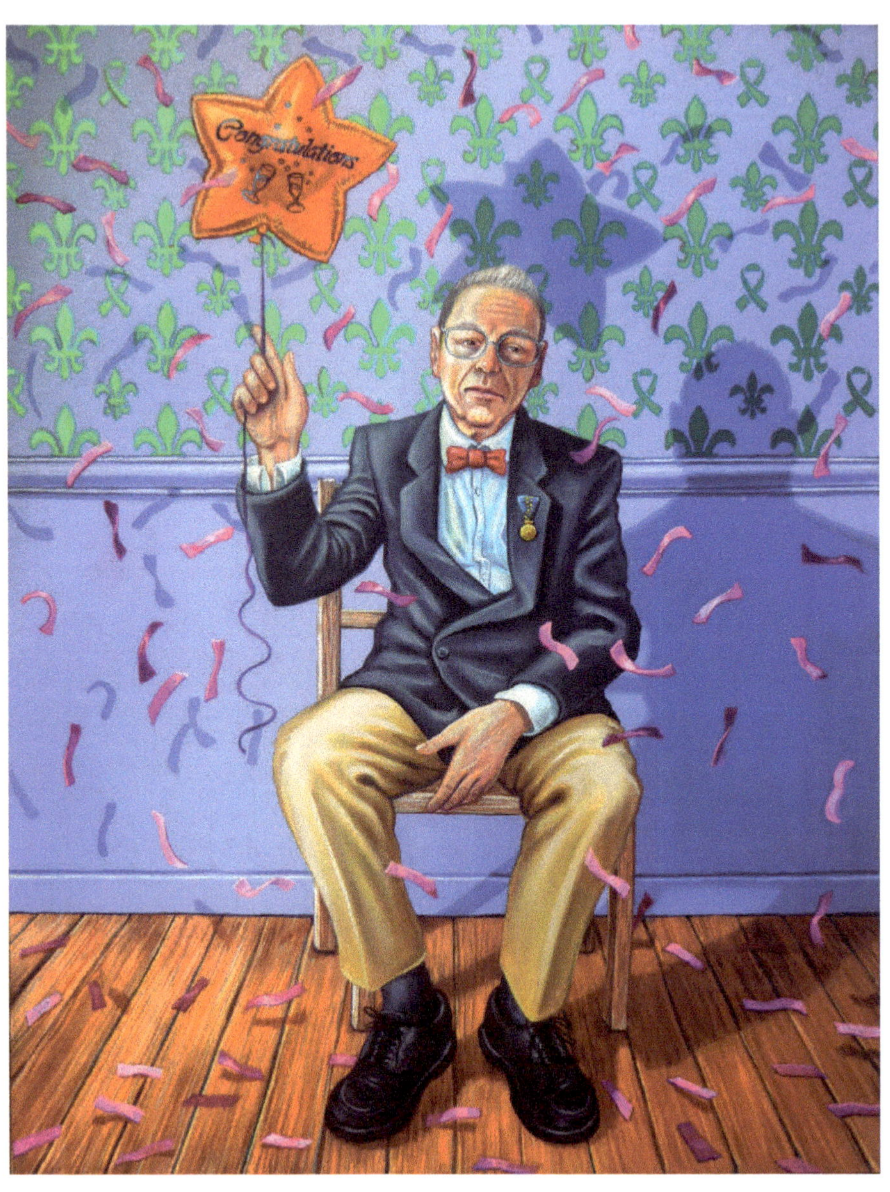

GUY JAMES WHITWORTH | LIFE

Guy James Whitworth

When I grow up I want to be Peter De Waal

When I grow up I want to be Peter De Waal. I've said that a few times to a few different friends over the past few months and it's very true … although I have no immediate plans to actually grow up.

*

Earlier this year I was really lucky to be offered a job as 'artist in residence' at The Pride in Place conference at Sydney University. It was a conference marking and celebrating the 40th anniversary of the very first Mardi Gras. I was required to sketch some of the original 78ers (and other people of note) who would be present or speaking at the event. It was a dream job and one I instantly accepted. Although to say I was a tad nervous was an understatement, all of these watercolour and pencil sketches were to be executed 'live,' as it were. I would be sitting front and centre, just a few feet away from the speakers as they spoke from their podiums, with my sketches clearly visible to the audience behind me. Now, let me tell you, while I like to think of myself as a confident sketcher and certainly not one to buckle under pressure, I am also certainly not fearless or foolhardy enough to avoid accepting that this *could all go horribly, horribly wrong.*

I asked the organisers if I could maybe meet one or two of the speakers before the conference, to get a couple of the sketches out of the way. This was also so I could settle on a particular style and colour palette (yes, I can sketch in a few different styles, it all depends on mood, state of mind and time allowances. Cocky, me? Hell yeah!). I was given two numbers to call, one for someone called (rather intriguingly) Gay Egg (more about that gorgeously inspirational individual another time) and a second called Peter De Waal. Peter's name was vaguely familiar, I was sure I'd read or seen something about him at some point. I spoke with him a few times and shortly after he invited me to his home, Chequerboard, which lead to me knocking on his door with a grubby tote bag of paints and pencils, not really fully understanding what the hell I was doing or what I'd really got myself into.

*

Peter de Waal is an absolute and utter bloody legend, literally, figuratively and really quite accurately. He has been a human rights activist from before I was born. He was one of the founding members of Australia's *Campaign Against Moral Persecution (CAMP)* and *Phone-a-friend* in the late sixties and seventies. In 1966 he met Peter Bonsall-Boone (aka Bon) who became his partner for the following 50 years, until Bon's passing last year. Scandalously, in 1972 the two Peters shared the first gay kiss ever aired on Australain TV on the ABC's Chequerboard program. Last year he was awarded the Order of Australia for services to the LGBTQI community (as was Bonsall-Boone, although sadly the medal came too late for it to be seen by him).

I knew all of this when I turned up at Peters door all those months ago, after Googling his familiar name, but I'd actually stopped researching after a few brief minutes when I realised how intimidating his achievements were.

You know that feeling when you meet somebody and they greet you and you feel that instant, wonderful, warm, easy feeling of '*we could be friends; I like you*'? Well, that is my overriding memory of what happened when I first met Peter. He is such a naturally warm and lovely man. He has deep set, sparkly eyes and a very easy smile. That someone could be so accomplished, respected and loved yet be so down to earth, practical and unpretentious is a wonder of the modern world. He is socially very kind and encouraging; he is a great listener and someone who rarely interrupts (I love people who don't interrupt, because, when I'm really babbling on about nonsense, I really don't want to be stopped).

It is often quite difficult to sketch someone you've only just met and get a very strong likeness. Capturing someone's likeness is also about capturing that person's character. We all guard ourselves socially and often present as someone whom we are not to people we don't know. However, with Peter I found him so easy to sketch. So much of what he is about is *being unguarded and open.*

I did four sketches that day. I was actually quite happy with the first one, but I didn't want to leave that quickly. So we sat and chatted, and I sketched, for probably a bit longer than we needed. In hindsight, I do remember him saying he was quite exhausted when I was leaving. I feel quite proud to say, Peter now has one of those sketches framed in his hallway.

*

I've seen Peter countless times over the past few months at different social events such as rallies. He even invited me, Gay Egg (it really is the *best ever* name) and a few of my mates over to his house for a private showing of the documentary '*Riot*'. The film documents the events surrounding the first Sydney Mardi Gras. That was a pretty special evening, watching 1978 with a couple of the real 78ers, and hearing all their drama and gossip from 'behind the scenes'.

I really wanted my partner Ryan to meet Peter. A few months ago I took him to see '*Chequerboard*'. I sat and sketched the outside of the house that had seen so much in the last 50 years as Ryan and Peter sat on the front balcony, obviously having a good old gossip about, well, only they know what. I, across the road and unfortunately out of earshot, fended off the neighbours who offered up their houses for a sketch. I'll be honest: that special day was slightly marred by my own grumpy jealousy of Ryan's quality time with my new friend!

I like to think Peter De Waal wants to be my friend almost as much as I want to be his and although I do still get a bit intimidated by all his amazing achievements, I just don't allow myself to think about them. And then the intimidation disappears. What really impresses me about him though is that after all his years (he just turned 80) he is never in any way bitter or jaded, but in the face of everything he has seen and done, he is so genuinely humble and lovely. I've said it before and I'll say it again: When I grow up I want to be Peter de Waal!

My only regret is that I missed out on meeting Bon. A few weeks ago I asked Peter if I could use the various sketches I have of him as the basis for a more studied painting. Luckily he agreed; I've been working on the piece since. It is a study not just of Peter, but of the painful and unnecessarily drawn out marriage equality postal vote, along with its process and outcome. It is a piece meant to be melancholic and bitter-sweet with an ever-so-gentle jab to the heart.

Bon passed away only a few months before marriage equality passed into law in Australia and couples of the same sex were finally allowed to marry. This meant this particular couple, who had tirelessly devoted their lives to campaigning for equality and same-sex marriage, were denied that union by timing (and by cancer too I suppose). I'm calling this painting 'Life'.

Steve RE Pereira

Freddie and me

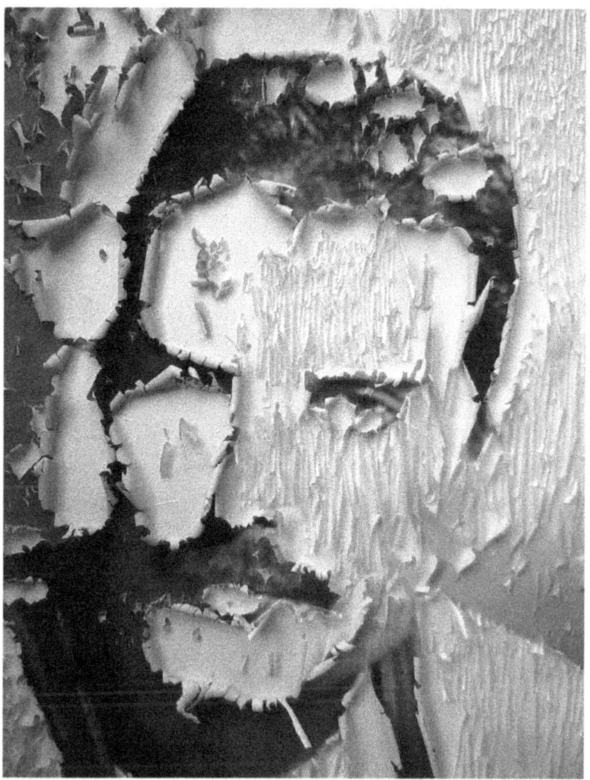

Adam Jones | Decaying photo of Freddie Mercury outside Mercury House, Stone Town, Zanzibar, Tanzania, 2013

We had a shared history Freddie Mercury and I, though we were born a generation apart. We were both born in Tanzania, I in Arusha in Tanzania in the shadow of Mt. Kilimanjaro, he on Zanzibar the clove-scented island that lies just sixty-eight km off the mainland coast. Both of us born into Indian migrant families but from outlier Indian communities. He was born Farrokh Bulsarara into the minority Parsi community of Iranian immigrants to India, followers of the Zoroastrian religion. I was born Steve Pereira into the Goan community; Portuguese colonial subjects othered in our Europeanised, Catholic ways. We were Indian but also, always something else as well.

We were both sent back from Tanzania to India to study in pseudo-British style boarding schools (He Anglican, me Catholic). We both emerged—me definitely, he arguably—very much one of Macaulay's notorious children; anglicised Indians 'a class of persons Indian in blood and colour, but English in tastes, in opinions, in morals (hmm …) and in intellect …' We both left Tanzania late in our late teens: he for the UK, me for Canada.

I gather from what I have read about Freddie that we had a similar response to our arrival in British land (or versions thereof). We thought we had arrived home only to discover that to most others we were just another Paki immigrant.

We diverged then. Farrokh Bulsarara morphed into the culturally ambivalent—*fair skin, striking aquiline features*—Freddie Mercury. I kept my culturally ambivalent name but took my darker skin, snub nose, round-faced, kinky haired self and became a born-again Indian playing with being a cultural activist. And yes, we were both gay, bi, whatever before I settled on gayness and it seems now that Freddie sort of did the same.

And that was how I first became aware of Freddie: I met his gayness before I knew anything else about him. When I discovered that he was *Indian*, and we had a shared background, I distinctly remember now over thirty years ago being winded, rendered breathless. I couldn't believe he was *one of us*.

*

My first distinct memory of Freddie was the Live Aid concert on 13 July 1985. It was Saturday evening in Mississauga, a suburban Toronto city where I lived my then schizophrenic semi-closeted existence with my parents and brothers. Straightness in the suburban home, gay abandon in the city.

That evening I was heading into the city to meet a group of friends at Boots, a bar in the heart of the gay village. When I came downstairs, my parents were watching the *Live Aid* special. 'Why?'

I asked. *Murder She Wrote,* and that ilk of TV was more their fare. 'It's about Africa', my father said like he was stating the bloody obvious. So starved were we all for any recognition in the western media of the worlds we came from that any mention of Africa snapped our attention. I looked cursorily at the TV screen as I was saying goodbye to them and then Freddie entered the screen and I was riveted to the spot.

I had never seen Freddie or Queen on screen before. We were fairly fresh off the boat in Canada having arrived five years earlier from Tanzania, which was then a closed off socialist state. We had had very limited access to Western pop culture. We had no TV. Effectively one radio station which was the *Voice of Kenya.* The movies we got were a diet of Chinese Kung Fu films, Bollywood melodramas and in a fist bump to African culture, American Blaxploitation films.

I had heard of the band and even had a cassette tape of Bohemian Rhapsody inherited from a Turkish roommate at university (who found the music bizarre). I loved the theatricality of it. I listened to the tape to destruction. I wasn't very much of a music fan—enjoyed pop and blues mostly—but music didn't captivate me the way that film, literature and theatre did—and I didn't have much of curiosity about Queen. Those pre-internet days, you had to make an effort to get information … I didn't care enough. Until *Live Aid,* when I saw Freddie perform.

Seeing Freddie on stage then for the first time was a revelation. It wasn't the performance—which even I knew enough to know was freaking awesome. What got me was the fact that he was *so gay.* That whole 'Village People look'. That aggressive, *unrepentant* bulge in his crotch. The prancing and the preening. How could he be so gay, and nobody said anything? Nobody that I knew anyway. My parents watching the show were oblivious, but then they thought the Village People were just men in costumes.

*

I was buzzing by the time I got to the club, walked past a dozen Freddie clones at the bar and met my friends in the back patio. They were largely gay South Asian men I had met and bonded with through support groups. We were South Asians from a variety of places in East and South Africa, India, Nepal, Pakistan, Bangla Desh, Sri Lanka, Trinidad, Guyana, Fiji; of various ages but mainly middle class and of a middling conservative, liberal bent. We were—and I write aware of the generalisation—church/mosque/temple-going, closeted gay men with jobs in the mainstream.

The guys I spoke to then about Freddie and Queen, knew of him and the music and even knew then of his Parsee, Zanzibari background, but played at being singularly unimpressed by that. I was flabbergasted. That strutting, preening butch queen, Rock & Roll god was Indian! Why were we not as South Asian queers shouting that out from the rooftops? We were fighting for visibility, for recognition from within our communities of the validity of our gayness and fighting for acknowledgement from the queer community of our cultural specificity. With Freddie we could say to everybody 'Look: we exist!' and 'Do a fucking double take because we can be superstars'.

The fact that Freddie never actually *said* he was gay was a problem, yes. But! Everything he did screamed *camp hyper-articulated gayness*. Did he really have to say the words? Really?

But in the essentialised identity politic that was the imperative of the time, apparently, that was the deal breaker for the queer community. For us South Asians it seemed to me there was another agenda at play as well. For some of us who survived by being on the down-low, Freddie Mercury was an embarrassment, and *the least said about him the better*. We didn't have any gays in *our* village, we said. Nothing to see *here*. So, when the press elided his cultural background or foregrounded his Iranian history as opposed to his Indian one in some kind of hierarchy of exotification, we didn't complain too much.

*

For me though, seeing Freddie strutting his stuff on that stage opened up a portal out of the Macaulay sarcophagus I had locked myself in. I was already chafing at my preppy, middle-class—yes bourgeois—family and social circle. I began drifting away towards a darker, much more sordid, but so much more exciting world. It wasn't just the sexual experimentation; it was the exhilaration of meeting people who committed themselves to their passions, who believed in nothing but themselves and often not even that, but who lived their lives with a desperate abandon and intensity. The question was in the zeitgeist: *Who Wants to Live Forever?* Tellingly the title of a posthumous documentary on Freddie.

But I was emerging into the scene too late. AIDs was devastating the gay scene. Dionysus was rapidly exiting stage left pursued by the orthodoxy of the new GLBTIQ community desperate to substitute the transgressive with the banal in order to sanitise the real. We were terrified of being tarred by the same brush that Joe Haines of the *Daily Mirror* used for his searingly-foul obituary of Freddie:

... *[he was] a man bent—the apt word in the circumstances—on abnormal sexual pleasures, corrupt, corrupting and a drug taker... his private life is a revolting tale of depravity, lust and downright wickedness.*

*

Bohemian Rhapsody, the Brian Singer film that started this memory trip, is everything the capital C *Critics* say of it: the screenplay is clichéd, the tropes tired, the characters one dimensional. However, it is much more than the sum of its parts. It is a deeply, moving and affecting film, saved by the music and Rami Malik's thrilling performance as Freddie, as the box office takings have proven. Once again Freddie has thumbed his nose at the orthodoxy and thwarted the Critics. I found the film deeply, lump in the throat, affecting. Two-thirds of the way through the film, as Freddie's illness was made apparent, I felt an overwhelming sense of loss. It wasn't just Freddie I was mourning. It was the loss of a time and the loss of all the truly radical people who through self-destructive hedonism were *on the cusp of reshaping* the way we dealt with our sexuality, our creativity, the notion of family and of relationships. That all died along with Freddie Mercury: that first Indian, British queer Rock and Roll star.

Jamie James & Quinn Eades

Queerdom

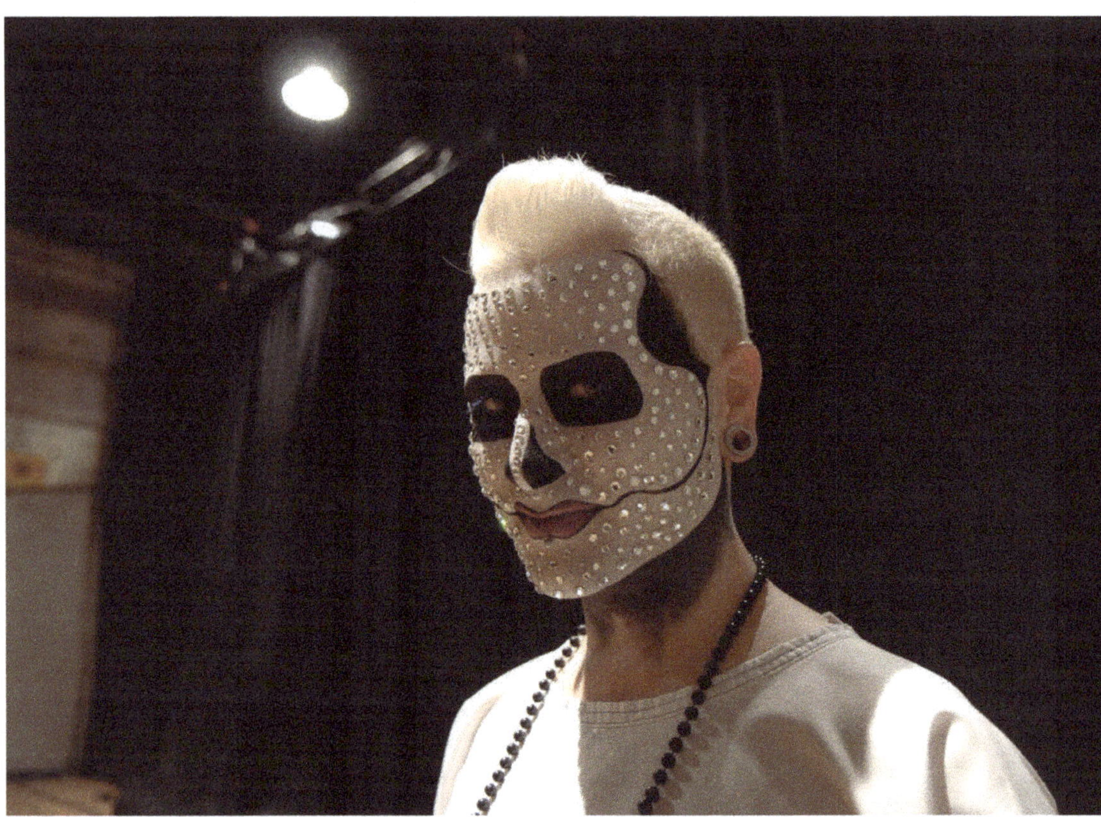

JAMIE JAMES | Pluto Savage, Quick and Dirty, Performance Space, Eveleigh, 2009

Jamie James is a genderbent photographer who has been working in queer and fringe performance spaces for three decades. Quinn Eades is a queer transmasc writer and poet. Jamie & Quinn are in love. The images and poetry are from their forthcoming book, *Queerdom*.

rough cut

Pluto is looking right through to the crux
jaw a fissure slit
alluvial deposits hidden in that curl of black
spitting hard diamonds
turning lips to lava
burning throat
temples
eyes
tongue
uvula
neck

later they will push injecting needles in through and out
wearing colossal heels and a crisp white coat

later they will stagger and shout
from their adamantine precipice
about blood borne diseases

expulsionsexcretionsexploitations

so I meet them here

learn to stand ankle deep in cinders and slag
to swallow magma laced memory
learn how not to forget

QUINN EADES

More from *Queerdom* on pp. 50, 78, 98, 110, 136.

Brigitte Lewis

Where did you go?

This is an excerpt chapter from a longer work, *Rage,* which is an exploration of Australian female identity and that the ideas we are taught are the truth at this moment in history. That, science is truth, that spirituality is irrational, that emotion is unreasonable and that using our reason to know is THE way. I knock on the door of each of these states of being in myself, embody them and find the limits of the ways I've created myself in the world and what learning to be rational has done to my ability to think, feel and experience myself as a person and as a woman.

I feel like I don't belong, like I don't know what anything means and I don't know how to be. I feel depressed. This is phenomenology; this is the result of using a method that instructs you to suspend your belief in everything you thought was true. Total utter fucking confusion. Do I sit and chant all day, chant and walk all day, chant all the time under my breath carrying *mala* beads and wearing a red dash of paint on my head like a devotee, do I practice slow breathing, making myself stay awake while listening to commentary on a CD meant to literally change how I think, what do I do now? *No fucking idea.* I'm fat as fuck and my *witness state* left me within a few days of being out of the ashram. All that work for a few days' pay-off. *Ugh. What a load of bullshit.* And *lies.* The Swami at Rikihia wasn't at Woodstock, it was someone else entirely! And our mantras are all the same. I can't forget or forgive that one, especially with their whole *honesty is integral to being spiritual* line. I spewed up my first glass of red wine and I've started hearing voices. Dead people.

*

It's March, I'm back in Melbourne, but I'm still recovering from my ashram stay in India two months later. I'm officially malnourished and overweight—is this even possible? I look like an African child with a bulbous stomach after I've eaten. Except mine is half fat and half something else altogether. My newly acquired naturopath says I've got candida. Not of the vagina (phew) but of the stomach, so I'm on a cocktail of probiotics and other supplements. I've been prescribed a diet of no sugar, alcohol, grains, gluten and pretty much every vegetable that I would normally eat. So it's all eggs, cabbage and herb mix from here on in. How bloody boring.

*

My dad's partner leaves the light on in the good room for her dead mother every night and I know when she arrives at our Melbourne family home. I can *feel* her. Yesterday my dad's best mate came over and his dead wife spoke to me and told me to tell him they would always be Shiva and Shakti and it was time for him to move on. I thought I was having psychotic flashback withdrawals from India and all the acid I'd consumed years earlier. But it turns out they did worship Shiva and Shakti—a construction worker with a beer gut and a penchant for gambling on horses and a skinny chain smoker who worshipped Hindu gods and goddesses. *Wtf?!* I was (almost) speechless. It's great to be back hanging with my brother, we play happy families as if we believe it, I get everyone healthy again, my dad loses so much weight he has to get his pants taken in. His partner says he's much happier when I'm around. I nod and smile. It's all for show I think, all for the status of people believing he is the ideal man. She drinks too much. He works too much. There is no intimacy there, just greetings and him falling asleep on the couch.

*

Next to me is an aspiring actress. The teacher who sits across from the two of us, Sally, is a large woman with sparkling blue eyes and silver-white hair. I'm about to begin a twelve-month psychotherapeutic acting course called *Character Creation* in the lounge room of her apartment in suburban Melbourne. We have met once before when she interviewed me for a place in the course. I sat across from her at a white plastic table with wonky chairs in an Asian restaurant on the corner of Elgin and Swanston streets in Carlton. Her eyes slicing into me making me feel naked, unsheathed, seen. She told me I was playing a part, that my persona held my emotion in. She's good I think to myself, *very fucking good.* But perhaps I'm pretty easy to read. A child's picture book in large lettering.

I'm nervous and excited all at once. Ready again to attempt to get out of my head and further into my body and my emotions, to grow myself up. Sally's place smells like essential oils and the faint aroma of her little dog, Luke. She gives me her self-devised booklet called *Character Creation* that will guide me through the next year. The first page is emblazoned with the words: *Challenge yourself to explore the full range of your expressive potential.* It's Sunday, and from now on all my Sundays will be spent in this room from 9:45am sharp until 7:00pm. Eight hours. Three semesters. Thirty weeks; $2,650. Over the year, I will be given six characters I'll have to learn to embody; six, because according to Carl Jung, there are six character types. I think it will be challenging, but I'll rise to the occasion. I always think that. Sally says no matter what we may think, everything in life is about ourselves, the self and our relationship to the self. I nod in agreement but I'm dubious. Life isn't just a solitary experience.

The first part of the class is psychoanalysis. Sally isn't trained to psychoanalyse me but my best friend David did her course and he raves about it and her. Sally's credentials are the usual pick-and-mix of new-age courses. She trained in voice dialogue and change consultancy which are based on various kinds of legit therapies like Gestalt but are run by people without the certified qualifications. Gestalt focuses on the here and now of experience and the self in relation to others. While Sally is not qualified to counsel or unravel me, she is a NIDA graduate—though in tech production, not directing as I expected. After NIDA she went on to study at the Drama Centre in London where she completed two years of the full-time actor's course. Following that, she came back to Australia and set up the Drama Studio in Sydney in the late seventies. After twelve years there she moved to Melbourne and she's been teaching Character Creation for the past ten years.

David—who is also Sally's best friend—is my lover now, not just my best friend. We're in an open relationship so he can be with men and I can be with women. It's complicated, but so far it's working out. I know I'll never desire him like I desire women, which makes me feel guilty, but I do love him deeply, more than I've ever loved anyone. I always wanted to be in an open relationship but before David I was never with anyone willing to forgo monogamy. This way I get the best of both worlds. The beautiful women and the intimacy of a best friend turned lover all rolled into one. But I've got to admit our sex life isn't the greatest. We have sex and it's fun. I'm just not *passionately engorged with lust* so it leaves me feeling too in control, too conscious, too human; *not enough animal.* 'Fun' isn't my definition of great sex, despite all the orgasms. Sally encourages us to have an open discourse about it and as a result we do more talking than two lesbians deciding on a sperm donor.

Our first class exercise with Sally is to identify our 'super-objective', what she defines as our reason to be or life goal. Every character we will inhabit over this course has one, she says. I decide that my personal super-objective, my reason to live, is to evoke change with my words. I feel way out of my depth next to the other student who attended the famed Victorian College of the Arts acting school. Sure, I've done spoken word poetry a few times, but I'm no actor, *not even close.* I tell myself that this will help me get into my emotions, that it's the logical next step. Sally tells me I need to learn to breathe into my body. At first I don't know what the hell she's talking about. But as I'm talking she stops me and says, 'Where did you go, what just happened? Why are you holding your breath?' And I look down and notice that I'm clinging to the couch. Fingers clenched. Breath held in. Her questions make me hold my breath tighter but when I realise what I'm doing I let out a laugh. At least here, I'm actually learning to feel my body, rather than control it like I did in India, or how I've learnt to do it as a rational thinker my whole life.

*

Sally's methods are unorthodox, to say the least. She uses her intuition and visual cues to unravel you, to get to the core of your dysfunctional patterns. Patterns that don't allow the actor to access any part of their being, whether it be emotional, psychological or physical. She says she's a transformational facilitator who enables the actor to recognise that every character lives inside them and that as human beings we have chosen to show up, to perform particular identities. We chose particular identities because they worked for us, our parents wanted us to be good at Maths or English, praised us for our dramatic skill and so we honed some parts of ourselves and put other areas aside. It makes sense to me.

When you're a thinker you learn to inhabit and embody your *self* in a particular way. If you're looking for it, it's easy to see when people are in their heads or don't want to be with what they're feeling. At least that's what Sally is teaching us. If I hold my breath, or cling to the couch, clip my words or my voice gets higher, I'm not here, I'm not in what she calls 'current reality'; I'm not fully in the moment. Other people tap their foot, or the colour of their skin changes, their eyes get narrow or wide, some cry, others play with their nails or watch. Anything to distract themselves from the intensity of the emotion they are feeling. The fact that we are taught we are not our emotions, but are often aligned with our minds, means—in the words of philosopher Glen A. Mazis—that a lot of people at this time in history experience their emotions as alien forces which are very powerful and before which they are helpless. I've always felt like this, always been pushed to feel this. And laughed at when I eventually crack. *Ha ha, you are weak. You're pathetic. You're just like your mum.* And my mum is a total fucking powerhouse.

*

The first character out of six I am given to embody is a woman called Mona. Sally tells me I need to get *user friendly* with not-knowing. Translated to plain English, this means I have to get out of my habit and desire to always want to know intellectually and be OK with just being, and not knowing. To let myself, as philosopher Judith Butler would say, be in the thrall of my emotions and others. Not an easy task, let me tell you right now. Sally chooses the characters she gives us based on what she thinks you need to embody, to get us feeling into the places we keep at arm's length. There's a lot of trust involved and I'm a control freak. And I'm also, on reflection, always looking for someone else to tell me the answers, the way, who I'm meant to be. But this, this deferring to another is on purpose.

Mona is an uber feminine, delusional woman who thinks she fathered James Dean's baby and is intent on making her community believe her. Think Marilyn Monroe-esque feminine. In acting parlance, her action is to make everyone believe she had James Dean's baby. Her objective is to be remembered as James Dean's greatest love and her super-objective is to live in a world where she is destined for fame and the fairy-tale of a one true love. Sally gives me this character to get me out of my masculine default position, to allow me to lose control. She orders me to start wearing dresses. To pretend I have oil everywhere so I roll into my skin, and to breathe into my body so I can start feeling all my emotions again. I revise my super-objective to be: *To live as though life were a beautiful woman wrapped around my face coming across my cheeks as I scream.* It sounds full on, I know, but I like full on. It makes me feel alive. And I love the taste of women. Sally talks about David constantly. If she were twenty years younger, they'd be together, I think silently to myself every time she mentions him… which is at least once a week.

Sally is constantly telling me to breathe into my body; that when anything challenging happens and I have to feel anything other than happiness or joy, I stop breathing. All so I feel as little as humanly possible. I leave my body, the flow of my breath for the safety of my head. When I get into this space, into my head like this, it's as if I am watching myself exist. So it's not that I don't feel, it's that I don't let myself feel much. Just like I was taught. Just like thinkers should be. Mind-centred and emotionally detached.

'Where did you go,' Sally asks?

What do you mean, I'm here, nowhere. I'm here, I say. And then I freeze up, my face drops and the tears come.

Jeff Herd

Interview

Melbourne singer-songwriter Jeff Herd released his first album Boy Down *earlier in 2018. Jeff is interviewed by* Bent Street *publisher Gordon Thompson.*

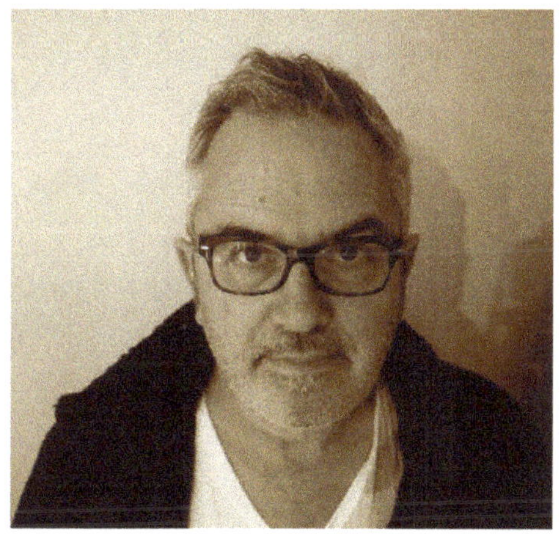

GT: Jeff, congratulations on *Boy Down.* It's a lyrically rich and playful collection, musically varied, and emotionally raw and punchy. I've been grooving along. Is this your first album?

JH: Thanks Gordon. I'm stoked that you like it. Yes, *Boy Down* is my first album. I've been a hobby musician since I was a kid, singing, playing guitar and piano. But this album really started with me leaving work in my mid-50s to pursue music. I went back to school and studied singing and then song-writing. My first song-writing teacher was Laura Jean, an amazing Melbourne singer-songwriter, and then Caroline Kennedy, an adventurous musician-artist, and others.

GT: How did that work?

JH: It was a workshop-type environment where we would bring songs or bits of songs in for feedback, and I found it really supportive and productive. Over 18 months, I wrote ten songs that seemed to fit together enough for me to try and make an album. So it's been a long-term dream that's finally happened.

GT: Did you have a plan for the album—some design method?

JH: It was a bit unplanned, but also full of aspiration. I'm a big fan of well-rounded albums. Once I'd finished writing the songs, I could see an autobiographical thread running through them, as well as a mix of musical styles. The bulk of the recording is John Lee, my producer, and me: a two-person band, so that helped cohere things. And I tried a lot of different sequences of the songs to reach the final order. So things eventually seemed to fall into place, a bit like solving a puzzle.

GT: Which of the songs, maybe in the studio, or just as song, gave you the most headaches? Which song, by contrast, seemed to write and record itself as if by magic?

JH: The lyric for 'Song for Mark Murphy' wrote itself. Mark was an amazing American jazz singer, a hero of mine, who died in October 2015. As I was reading an obituary, there was a reference to his partner, Eddie, who had died in 1990. I was blown away that Mark was gay and I hadn't known. I was studying jazz vocal at the time, and the jazz world felt pretty straight. The presence or absence of relatable role models really affects your sense of possibility. So I poured all that out in the lyric.

GT: There are some lovely lines there—and a great setting: 'Bebop against the silence/ trust the deeper world will channel your song'. … And any 'difficult' songs?

JH: 'White Feathers', about masculinity and courage, proved to be really difficult in the studio. Musically it's built on simple piano chord pattern I played as a kid, but it also switches from waltz-time to 4/4 then back again. And the lyrical mood is fairly dreamy and subterranean. We tried and then dropped bass guitar and drums, and decided to let the piano part lead the arrangement. We worked on a lot of layers: synth strings, clarinet sounds, classic moog sounds. John recorded the rain on the roof of the studio and added that. I wasn't sure it was all going to work, but it ended up being very atmospheric and I'm really happy with it.

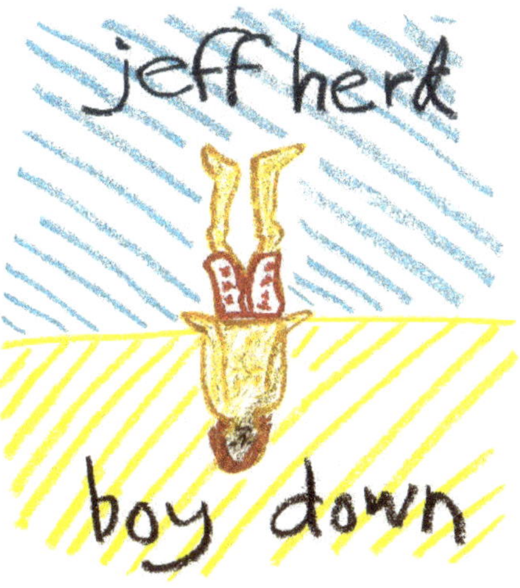

GT: You've mentioned the jazz influences here. I must admit it didn't strike me, not at first, as a 'jazz' album—the cover, the guitars and synths, the alt country. But then on other listenings I realise it's dripping with jazz. I've shared the album with friends who have noted that it reminds them of The Whitlams, and I'm picking up traces of My Friend the Chocolate Cake, Barroworn, not to mention the Magnetic Fields … but what are some of your other musical influences?

JH: Influences and loves are hard to untangle. On the radio as a kid, I loved the Beatles, Stones, all sorts of pop music, Daddy Cool. Early seventies singer-songwriters—Joni Mitchell, Neil Young—made a big impact on me. I loved getting lost in the personal worlds they created. Later, Elvis Costello, The Velvets and Lou Reed's early solo work, Jeff Buckley, Massive Attack, Gillian Welch. These are all incredible talents, and I'm not claiming any big links here. But I had the Beatle's anthemic chorus style in mind when creating the background vocals for 'Boy Down' and 'Illuminate'. I had Neil and Joni in mind when writing the piano chords for 'Wild Freesias'. Jeff Buckley influenced the bridge of 'Pillow/Hammer'. 'Can't Hold On' started as a Lou Reed-style three-chord song before it turned alt-country. So my decades of listening pleasure also gave me some reference points to aim for. And more recently, fearless queer artists like Taylor Mac and Justin Vivian Bond—who I name-check in 'Faggot Artists'—have been inspiring.

GT: So my attempts to find an 'alt-Melbourne' ethos have fallen in a heap!

JH: Yeah, sorry about that! As a late starter, it's true I didn't incubate within a specifically Melbourne scene. But I did connect up more with Melbourne indie and jazz music culture through going back to school. I hadn't known of Laura Jean or her music before she taught me, and she's a favourite artist of mine now. For recording, I worked firstly with Simon Grounds, and then, for the album, John Lee. Both Simon and John have long careers as producers in the Melbourne indie music scene. So I connected up through the work.

GT: I'd like to talk a little more about the lyrics. I really enjoyed the specific autobiographical elements, but you also make the stories resonate in broader ways—'Wild Freesias' talks of childhood trips to the Barwon Heads, sleeping on the trip home with your head in Mum's lap, dreamy childhood; but suddenly there are undercurrents beckoning—a wild wintry ocean. Mum and Dad reappear in 'Faggot Artists', along with other 'heteronormative' constraints, but it's the wider world of New York gay artists who will help you dream new dreams and maybe escape what Geelong represents: 'In Geelong I read New York faggot artists /and began to dream new dreams.'

JH: I had fun name-checking Geelong and New York Faggot Artists in the same line. The big light-bulb lesson I learned about song-writing is the key thing you have to offer is your self, your specific life experience, including your geography. So I was emboldened to write about the beach, growing up, school, family, feeling isolated, coming out, desire, getting older. And aspects of the broader world that I find important: the extraordinary contribution of queer artists to culture and progress, Aboriginal culture, climate change. And there was also a hunger to make my song, a song that I hadn't heard a lot of. Now, let's turn the table: what motivates or inspires your music-making?

GT: I feel like giving a Billy Elliot answer '*Was there any particular aspect of ballet that captured your imagination?*' '*Yes, the dancin'*. Basically I love the whole feel of music. I love being inside it—I love its flavours, the colours, how it moves. That's the key motivation … I also enjoy words and wordplay, which is a different set of sensations, but it means I write songs rather than instrumental music. At the moment I'm working on an album of settings of the poetry of Thomas Hardy, but using British post-punk as the design method—so it sounds a bit like New Order and Billy Bragg crossed with Vaughan Williams.

JH: That's an alluring description of your current project, which I'm really looking forward to. I share your interest in words, which also drives me to song-writing rather than instrumental music. My usual writing method is to start with lyrics, which can often begin with a phrase that jumps into my head: 'Boy Down', 'Full of Want', and 'Can't Hold On' started that way. Lyrics suggest rhythm, tempo, and genre and my melodies tend to flow out of them.

GT: Now, spinning the table back your way, what next for Jeff?

JH: *Boy Down* is out and I'm preparing an album launch, and maybe some other gigs. I'm writing again—I had a big break, but I'm back on the horse and that feels good. A friend and I have an exploratory writing project scheduled for later in the year.

Checking out Melbourne music is a constant—jazz, great singers like Emma Donovan, Mama Alto, Michelle Nicolle. I'll probably mainly head to a second album, which will take a while to pull together.

Search for Jeff Herd and Boy Down on Spotify, Bandcamp or iTunes.

Adrienne Kisner

Young Adult Fiction in #20gayteen

Tiffany Jones in conversation with Adrienne Kisner

Adrienne Kisner is the author of Dear Rachel Maddow, *a novel in which the protagonist Brynn Harper watches the Rachel Maddow Show daily and writes its star an email. Maddow responds, setting Brynn off on a frenzy of further emails about her first serious girlfriend, her brother Nick's death, her passive aggressive mother and student representation at school.*

TJ: Many people passionately watch Rachel Maddow's political news analyses, especially now as a guide to the problems of the Trump Administration … I am finding myself relating to how your book's main character Brynn Harper watches Maddow daily! Despite (or because of?) Maddow's political PhD she really simplifies complex concepts behind news events; I imagine young people finding her helpful in understanding current crises. And, dashing. So the basic concept behind this book is very timely and relatable: a young lesbian protagonist Brynn Harper receives a response to her Rachel Maddow fan mail, and then starts writing Rachel a series of confessional emails … Are you or people in your life daily Maddow fans?

AK: I definitely am! I started watching by accident and kept watching because Rachel became like a really informed friend I had never met. I dragged people in my life along with me and now I think several still watch out of habit.

TJ: I dearly love that part of the basic premise of the book is that Brynn writes, but does not send, these emails to Maddow. Ahhhh the awkward, tragic yearning for connecting with our idols! I felt voyeuristic in reading such personal fan-mail, until I saw Brynn's teacher was reading it too … this narrative device made me *even more embarrassed* for Brynn (at her naïve self-exposure) but less embarrassed for myself (since she knew adults would be viewing her effort at connecting to Rachel). Who were your idols growing up, and why did you connect to them?

AK: LOL, I had a few and they were random. I rather liked 'Deanna Troi' from *Star Trek: TNG*, because I am as cool as they come. She could feel people's feelings! I always wondered why she was the only psychological professional on a ship for thousands, though. That's pretty bad ass. I also admired a man named 'David Horowitz', who had this consumer advocacy show that informed people on advertising versus reality. I loved that guy. And finally Ann M. Martin—creator of *The Baby-Sitters' Club*. She was the first writer with whom I felt really connected. All of her work just spoke to me. They were all a mix of empathy, advocacy, and fun. How could young me not want to emulate them?

TJ: I met some of my idols; dubious choice. Our own fabrications about our idols can be the part we had most connected to. Did you ever meet any idols in the flesh?

AK: I once met Rainbow Brite when I was eight. I was horrified when she was a large, polyester facsimile of a person who was not at all magical. Since then I've made it a point to avoid the famous.

TJ: What do you see as the main value of idols for their younger (or any) LGBTI fans?

AK: Idols, like any character we know but don't quite, point out how we might be in the world. What is possible, someone to whom we can ideally aspire. Are some idols famous for not really doing anything (I won't name names)? Yes. But they provide a window into another reality, because sometimes our own isn't that great. That is valuable.

TJ: The plot of *Dear Rachel Maddow* explores how Brynn becomes aware of oppression in her life and tries to get active in the political world of her school. Were you politically active at school?

AK: I was on the paper. I wrote snarky little op-eds that got me called into the principal's office more than once. But I WILL say that the school orchestra was forced to practice in a bathroom for a semester. I wrote about that, and they moved us. I was a volunteer in an in-patient child psychiatric unit, I convinced people to fundraise for different causes with me. I tried in small ways. I wasn't very good at it, as I was largely afraid of talking to people. But I always believed you had to try to push yourself out of your comfort zone to make a change.

TJ: Your book's focus on youth activism is well-timed given US youth are featuring strongly in 2018's political activism in and beyond schools—in protests on transgender youth bathroom access; #20gayteen; Black Lives Matters; Women's Marches, March for Our Lives campaigns … and now on the mistreatment of immigrant children. Is this cohort more politically engaged, or more affected by recent political decisions?

AK: I think that it is easier to see and thus experience the injustices of others. These things are on film and widely distributed, instead of just talked about in marginalized communities. I hope it continues to wake the sleeping.

TJ: The book comments on some key barriers to political engagement in a clever way. How are these barriers playing out in the US at the moment?

AK: I worry that the American experiment is crumbling. It is giving way to the dark impulse of totalitarianism because of fear. The free press is under attack, the rule of law is under attack. But I also think hope is not lost. People are protesting. People have lived with dystopian fiction long enough that we can't say that we weren't warned. People will continue to resist. I just hope it's enough.

TJ: You teach people to write; this came through in the witty authenticity of the teacher's comments on Brynn's writing development in the book … and Brynn's resistance to being edited. We have many creative types reading *Bent Street* journal; what advice features in your current writing lessons?

AK: You have time to write. Yes, yes. I'm sure your car broke down and your partner broke up with you and your basement is filled with feral cats. That's life. It you want to write, you can do it. Ten minutes at a time every other day will finish a novel eventually. Not only can you do it—you should. The world needs your story. Also, learn to format dialogue properly. Break the rules if you want, but know them first. And know your character as well as you can—that is where the plot will come from.

TJ: Your book is categorised as 'Young Adult/ YA Fiction'. Whilst categories aid in indicating *reading difficulty*, separation of fiction into 'adult' and 'YA' genres feels artificial; kids can love adult books and adults can love 'YA fiction'. I use YA fiction with thousands of pre-service teachers (adults), who are often already reading it! We perhaps start reading with a 'young adult imagined reader' alongside us; a great book evaporates that device. Are you aware of your adult fans, or adult YA fans broadly?

AK: I would not call myself a fan of any fiction outside of that for younger readers; save Elizabeth Gilbert (I'm a sucker for Elizabeth Gilbert). Adult fiction is packed with middle aged angst, and I can just get that anytime I want in my daily life, thanks. Kids haven't given up on the impossible, they allow for the imagination to have the most say. They will also call a writer out for inauthenticity. So their books are just better written. If adults read my work for similar reasons–hello, readers. You are my people.

TJ: What is different about writing YA fiction versus fiction intended for adults?

AK: I'm not sure how to write for adults. Maybe take the fun and possibility out of things? Ha! I kid. (Kind of). I'm always baffled why someone would *write for adults on purpose.* Is there more money in it? That seems unlikely. Do they enjoy being an adult? Adults can stay up later and spend money the way they want, but I've found that just leaves me tired …and broke. BORING.

TJ: Recently Australia has had inquiries into the 'age-appropriateness' of texts on LGBTI topics for young people. Perhaps it's a fabricated concern to provoke conservative outrage for our elections … Does your work garner this sort of critique?

AK: I haven't gotten that. My character swears a lot, so I don't know that it ever makes its way into the hands of really young readers. But casting LGBTI content as age-inappropriate is just another way of trying to censor it. You aren't helping kids by keeping the world from them. They are the world, what benefit is there in hiding them from themselves?

TJ: Wonderful points. It's a shame YA writing experts are overlooked in these debates, in favour of people lacking expertise on LGBTIs or writing. On to your new work; what are you writing now?

AK: My current book is about two younger kids who live in a high rise dormitory. It's basically a love letter to my own children, who have always lived in a dorm because of my job. I don't know if anyone will think it as funny as I do, but I crack myself up every day while writing it. I get funny looks in the library. It's better than *Dear Rachel Maddow* or my second book out next year, *The Confusion of Laurel Graham*—I burst out crying once or twice with those. I should probably just write at home.

See further in bent street 2 for an extract from *Dear Rachel Maddow.*

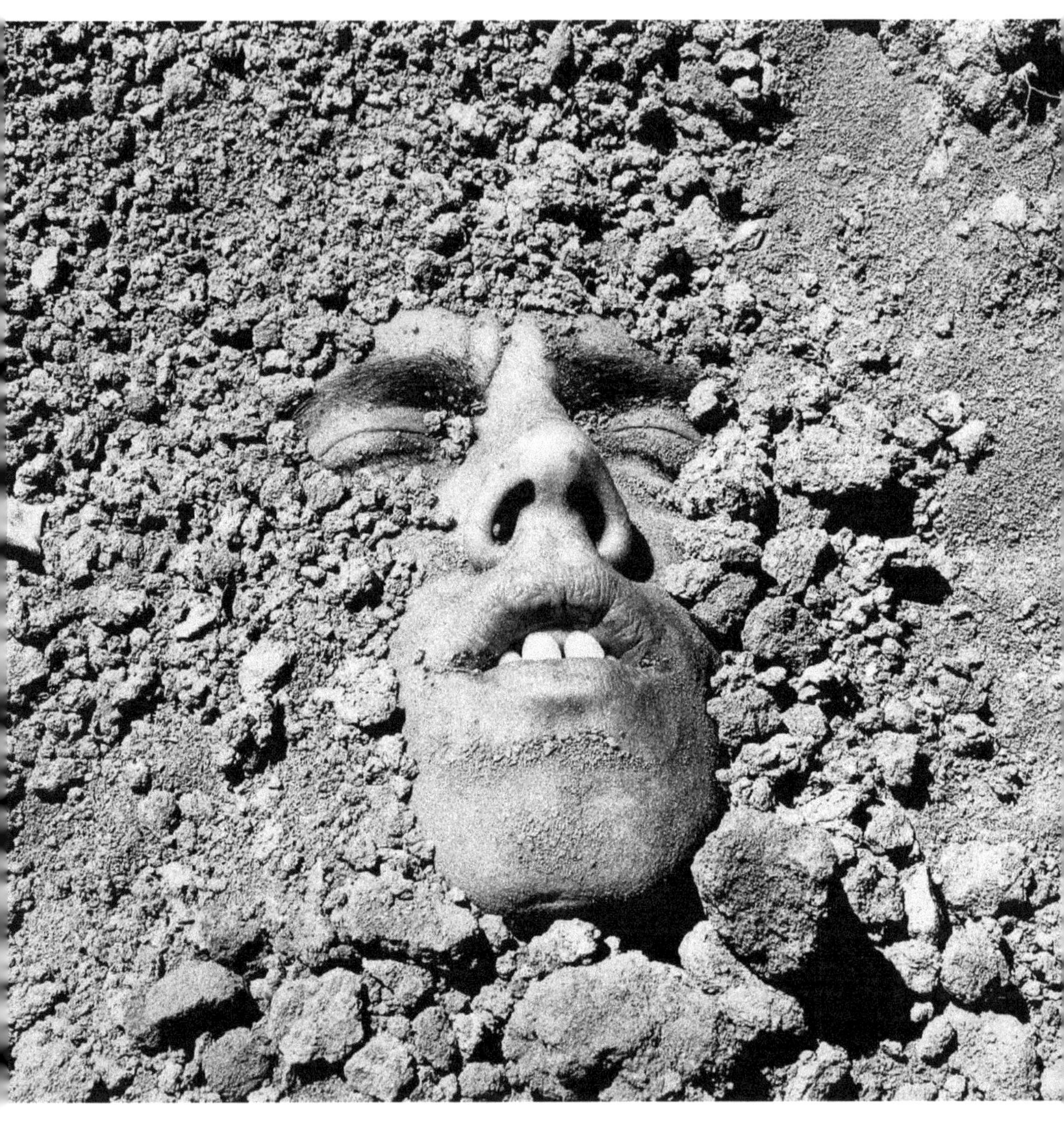

DAVID WOJNAROWICZ | UNTITLED (FACE IN DIRT) 1990-1993

Marcus O'Donnell

David Wojnarowicz's lips

1

The Song of Solomon, the bible's surprisingly erotic master poem, begins with a kiss.

'Let him kiss me with the kisses of his lips …'

This astounding poem is filled with the sensory world of the lover: the smell of him, the caught sight of his nakedness, the taste of him; but it is here with the kiss that it begins. With the lips.

When our lips part, what is that space between?

What do our lips remember? What do they long for? What do they wet?

2

David Wojnarowicz had beautiful lips. Full, fleshy, seductive.

In a reverie that might be a dream, a memory, a fiction, Wojnarowicz writes of wandering through a labyrinthine structure following the hint of a boy: first it is the wind at his heels that blows past as a door opens and shuts, then the hum of his red jacket in the distance. Then the lure of his lips:

'I could feel his lips against mine from across the room, tasting reefer or milk on them as he disappears through the square hole in the ceiling …'

Then he falls right into the taste of him.

'Like water falls from the sky I leaned in close and slid down and unsnapped his jeans button by button using only my teeth. He was wearing no underwear and I peeled back the flag of his trousers, his dick falling neatly out to rest on my lips …'

What do our lips anticipate? What do they follow? What do they consume?

3

I can't remember when I first heard of David Wojnarowicz. I probably first saw his artwork in the 1994 National Gallery of Australia exhibition on art and AIDS, *Don't Leave Me This Way*.

I would have read pieces of his writing a few years earlier in anthologies that were profiling new transgressive queer writing dealing with sex, bodies and marginal lives. Kevin Killiam an emerging queer poet at that time, said they were aiming for 'a new kind of storytelling' where 'poetry, theory, gossip, and porn intermixed in order to accommodate [and] treat the big issues of the day and our own tenuous hold on that'.

Wojnarowicz started out in the 70s with the ambition of being a poet, but he also drew obsessively. He had sketched and collaged since he was a kid. But his urge to assemble and make visible whole imaginative worlds could not be confined to the page. Over a number of years he become a visual artist working across sculpture, painting, film and installations: an artist who also wrote rather than a poet who sketched.

Wojnarowicz's *Self Portrait in Twenty Three Rounds,* which begins his 'memoire of disintegration', *Close to the Knives*, also made it into the *Penguin Book of Gay Short Stories,* which was published the same year as the NGA show. The story begins with an image of his conception and meanders through images of sex, violence and survival culminating in a haunting image fusing innocence and death. Wojnarowicz, as a kid hustler, putting his clothes on after sex, and the guy 'says he loves the way my skeleton moves underneath my skin when I bend over to retrieve one of my socks'.

It is in these kinds of compelling images that Wojnarowicz displayed his unique poetic melancholy, a sensibility that bumped right up against death with a longing that tipped back into life.

4

After no contact for many years, Wojnarowicz met up with his brother Steven, who had chanced upon a magazine feature about David and suddenly realised his little brother had become a somewhat famous artist. The first thing David said, with virtually no preliminaries, was: 'You know I was a child prostitute'.

No preliminaries. That's how Wojnarowicz's art functions. An unmediated witness to what is happening. He wanted to show life beyond what he called 'the preinvented world'—the world that was structured by corporations, overbearing governments, churches and years of unquestioning culture.

'I wake up every morning in this killing machine called America,' Wojnarowicz says on one of his tapes, 'and I'm carrying this rage inside like a blood-filled egg.'

They are also words that are repeated on a print *Untitled (ACT-UP), 1990,* that was featured in the 1994 NGA show.

'I'm carrying this rage inside like a blood-filled egg and there is a very thin line between the inside and the outside, a thin line between thought and action … and as each T-cell disappears from my body it's replaced by ten pounds of pressure ten pounds of rage and I focus that rage into non-violent resistance but that focus is starting to slip …'

Redemption, where do we find it? Shame how do we let it go? Rage what do we do with it? What is that skin thin membrane between life and death?

5

Wojnarowicz died of complications from AIDS in 1992, the year I decided to go to art school. But his work has continued to both cause scandal and to grow in importance. This year his career has been celebrated with a major retrospective at New York's Whitney Museum: *History Keeps Me Awake At Night.*

The title of the Whitney show —— taken from one of the artist's paintings—immediately tells you what kind of artist Wojnarowicz is. As curators David Breslin and David Kiehl insist in the introduction to the exhibition's beautiful catalogue:

'Wojnarowicz's work is ultimately an ethical practice. That is the work participates in the philosophical tradition of inquiring about, systematizing, and defending concepts of right and wrong conduct. As such, the practice is one that asks that most naïve and yet pressing question: How should we live?'

As a number of reviewers have noted, the location of this tribute is ironic as the new Whitney represents the ultimate gentrification of a corner of New York that was once the dishevelled cruising ground of gay men, street hustlers and drug users. The location of very differently lived lives than those who occupy it today. Wojnarowicz not only played there, but began his art-making there: graffitiing the walls of the long-gone cruise warehouses at the New York piers.

Born in 1954, Wojnarowicz was the product of a family that his biographer Cynthia Carr calls 'beyond dysfunctional'. His father was an abusive alcoholic and his mother seemed unable to care for either herself or her children. David ended up living on the streets for a number of years as a teenager and the danger and abuse that he experienced there became a crucial lens through which he viewed the world.

He told Carr that he used to long for acceptance from others but then he realised he didn't fit.

'Then he began to value the way he didn't fit in. He realised that his uneasiness with the world was where his work came from.'

How do our lips fit together? How do we prize them apart?

6

Two boys lip-locked and reaching into one another stand waist deep in a swirling, spurting pool of dark water. They float as stencilled outlines at the center of *Fuck You Faggot Fucker (1984)* a key work Wojnarowicz created for an early show.

Their bodies tattooed with a collage of maps.

Where will we go with each other, they seem to ask. How will we find each other across space and time? Where is that one point where we get lost: the latitude and longitude of love?

Surrounding them four photographs. In three corners the repeated image of David and a friend, naked in an abandoned building. In the other corner another friend, in a different abandoned scene, posing as Saint Sebastian. Below the boys, a graffiti scrawl: Fuck you faggot fucker.

The stencil of the lip-locked boys recurs several times in Wojnarowicz's work. He copied it onto the letter that Peter Hujar, his mentor and one time lover, had received diagnosing him with AIDS. Wojnarowicz again used the image in a quilt panel he did for another friend who had died around the same time as Hujar.

The simple lines of the stencil capture the way a kiss is both the touch of lips and the twist of bodies, the tilt of my head jigsawing against yours, the reach of my arm around you, the turn of your torso.

Why did Wojnarowicz use this image of two boys kissing to memorialise Hujar's diagnosis and death from AIDS? Was it the intensity of their love he was memorialising? Was it a celebration of desire against the threat of death? Was it the kiss, the pull, of death itself?

Wojnarowicz was no stranger to the pull of death. As a young boy he used to hang over the roof's edge, eight stories high, just to see what it was like.

He told the art critic Lucy Lippard that when he was first diagnosed with HIV he felt 'this abstract sensation'.

'Something like pulling off your skin and turning it inside out and then rearranging it so that when you pull it back on it feels like what it felt like before, only it isn't and only you know it … the first minute after being diagnosed you are forever separated from what you had come to view as your life or living, the world outside the eyes. The calendar tracings of biographical continuity get kind of screwed up … the entire landscape and horizon is pulling away from you in reverse order to spell out a psychic separation.'

The kiss pulls us back, we put on the skin of another, we twist, we turn into one another. In annotating Hujar's diagnosis letter, Wojnarowicz, date stamps this moment—this calendar tracing of biographical continuity—with love.

7

If you google David Wojnarowicz, one of the first images you will find is of his lips. Lips sewn shut in protest.

It is a defiant image, taken by his friend Andreas Sterzing, for the poster of a film about the AIDS epidemic, *Silence = Death*, by Rosa von Praunheim.

Wojnarowicz was the subject of censorship on a number of occasions, but the slogan Silence = Death, used by AIDS activists, protested, not explicit moments of censorship, but the silencing of lives through the government's, and in the context of 1980s America, specifically President Regan's refusal to speak about or act on AIDS. In this graphic image Wojnarowicz makes visible the silencing, not just of dissenting speech, but of queer loving, queer sexuality and queer dying.

Wojnarowicz's work arises out of the silence of his childhood, when his sense of his own strangeness, had sewn his young lips shut.

'When I was a kid I discovered that making an object, whether it was a drawing or a story, meant making something that spoke even if I was silent. As an adult, I realize if I make something and leave it in public for any period of time, I can create an environment where that object or writing acts as a magnet and draws others with a similar frame of reference out of silence or invisibility.'

How do we conjure each other out of silence? How do we coax each other to see?

8

About a year before he died, Wojnarowicz took a final road trip with friend and fellow artist Marion Scemana, with whom he'd had a close but tempestuous relationship. At the Chaco Canyon, in northwest New Mexico, he asked Marion to help him create one of his final and one of his most arresting pieces.

They dug a hole in the harsh dry earth and buried David so that just his eyes, nose, lips and chin were visible, his dusty features emerging from the rough earth. Here his lips are parched and dry.

Marion stood over him and took a photograph.

Wojnarowicz, was self-consciously creating his own death mask. Kissing his own lips goodbye.

'We walked back to the car, and we sat without saying a word,' Scemana told Cynthia Carr. 'He didn't turn the car on. We stayed like this for a few minutes, and then we held hands.'

9

Sharing a stage with him, at one of his final public appearances, Kathy Aker called David Wojnarowicz 'a saint'; and in an interview around that time Nan Goldin called him 'kind of the moral conscience of our time'. His friends who had often been subject to his rages and tantrums might have felt differently. His boyfriend, Tom, said that he just laughed.

But if the posture of the saint is to give their life for others, Wojnarowicz was a kind of saint: a gritty, sexy, imperfect one. As Cynthia Carr says in the introduction to her biography: 'He had decided to let everything in his emotional history become part of his palette.'

He was part of a radical new way of being queer in public, having sex in public, and during the most harrowing years of the AIDS epidemic, struggling to live and often dying in public. He exposed himself and he refused to let others turn away.

In a work he made for his final show, *Untitled (When I Put My Hands On Your Body)*, 1990, he selected a photograph he had taken of an Indian burial mound, skeletons emerging out of the earth, in the same way that his face had emerged out of the earth in the Chaco Canyon, and he printed over it a startling poetic text about the body, about death, about love.

It begins with touch and tenderness.

'When I put my hands on your body on your flesh I feel the history of that body. Not just the beginning of its forming in that distant lake but all the way beyond its ending.'

The warm felt body begins to slip away, the mortal lover begins to dissolve as flesh falls from bone. The poet asks himself what he might do, what he might give, how me might save another.

'If I could attach our blood vessels so we could become each other I would. If I could attach our blood vessels in order to anchor you to the earth to this present time I would. If I could open up your body and slip inside your skin and look out your eyes and forever have my lips fused with yours I would.'

What might we see out of the eyes of another? What might we taste with their lips? How might we become their kiss?

The exhibition History Keeps me Awake At Night, *Whitney Museum of American Art, New York, July 13-September 30 2018, is richly documented in an archive at https://whitney.org/Exhibitions/DavidWojnarowicz and includes extensive recordings of seminars and interviews about Wojnarowicz and the era.*

Note on Sources

All biographical details and quotes from Cynthia Carr are from her 2012 biography: *Fire in the Belly: The Life and Times of David Wojnarowicz*. Bloomsbury Publishing USA.

All quotes from Wojnarowicz, unless otherwise indicated are from *Close to the knives: A memoir of disintegration*, originally published in 1991 and reissued by Canongate Books 2017.

Kevin Killiam quoted in Crandall Maxe, 2017. Congratulations, You're a New Narrative Subject. https://openspace.sfmoma.org/2017/12/congratulations-youre-a-new-narrative-subject/

David Breslin and David Kiehl (eds), *History Keeps me Awake At Night*, 2018, Whitney Museum of American Art, Yale University Press.

Lippard, L.R., 1994. Passenger on the Shadows. *In Brush Fires in the Social Landscape, Aperture*, (137), pp.6-25.

Goldin Nan, 1994. Love Sex Art and Death. *In Brush Fires in the Social Landscape, Aperture*, (137) https://aperture.org/blog/david-wojnarowicz-and-nan-goldin/

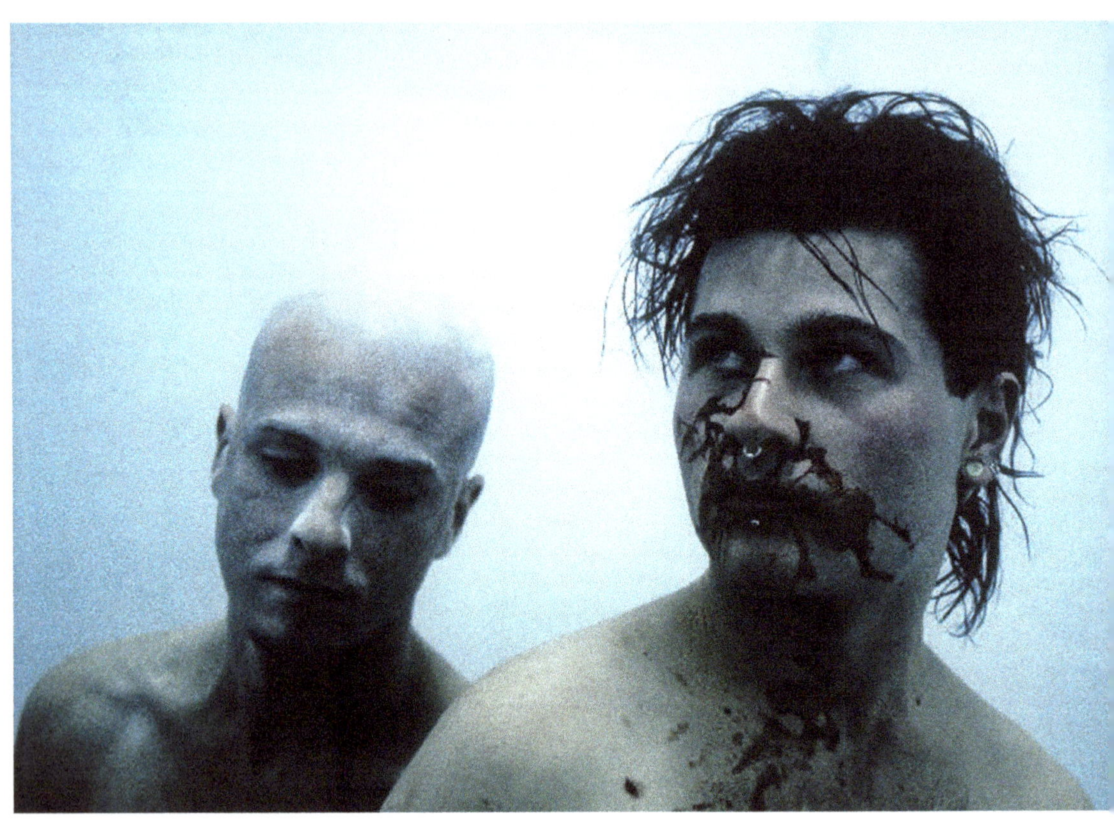

JAMIE JAMES | Pluto Savage & Lotus, Performance Positive, Pride Centre, Surry Hills, 1999

what we bring with us

in 1999 PrEP was 13 years away from NSW
19 years away from the PBS
poor queers dying but the last ones
to swallow that pill

in the wait chemical euphoria illegal (still)
cop hands in our pockets our chests our mouths
in our arses under a grey moon setting under
pupils dilated under an eaten morning under
a blissing dawn

in the wait turning ghosted and blue under
fluorescent light on Tungsten slide film

needled lips bloody
skull haloed
brows mothbrushed and overhung

from one: *that messy bitch is Pluto*
through and through

from the other: LOVE scarred across this chest
out of frame carrying skinwriting
keloid
text

what we bring with us

to our parties
to our dirtwet graves
to this turned page

QUINN EADES

Jennifer Power
Interview

A lesson in Queer: interview with a lesbian mum

Jennifer Power is an Australian academic, social commentator and researcher of LGBTIQ concerns. Her PhD explored gay activism and HIV in Australia and she's had a long association with same-sex and gender diverse communities through her work at the Australian Research Centre in Sex, Health and Society and The Bouverie Centre, both at La Trobe University. Jennifer has published many works about same-sex parented families in Australia in both academic journals and in social media forums. She is a mum of two young children and is connected with the rainbow families community in Victoria. In this interview with Henry von Doussa, she talks candidly about how her queer identity is shaped by, and shapes, her work as an academic, her relationships, her parenting and her desire to interrogate norms.

Henry von Doussa: Jen, I want to start by asking you a bit about what it's like working in the queer family space as a researcher and academic having to research an area that is personal for you; that is your life?

Jennifer Power: There is always a tension for queer academics doing work in sexuality or gender studies because your personal life is part of the story in some ways. For me, being a queer parent and doing research on same-sex parented families has made me really think about how and when (and when not) to insert my own life into my academic work. But there are certain criticisms levelled at queer academics. I've been named on right wing websites saying, in effect: '*this is a queer parent so don't trust her research*'. There's this assumption that if you're a queer parent you can't be producing reliable research on the subject. And there's an assumption that, as a queer academic, you must have a political agenda, so therefore your research is unreliable.

Obviously, that sort of critique is not levelled at say a cisgender straight man who's working in men's health. No-one assumes he's got an agenda because he wants men to be healthy. But because you're on the margins you get identified as such. And because you're in a political field, it's a sort of tension you need to navigate. Usually I argue that if your work is reliable and rigorous and transparent, then it just doesn't matter who you are personally. And I stand by that. But I think that's a pity in some ways because sometimes it's really powerful to draw on your own life and it can genuinely inspire research and writing.

HD: So what do you do, Jen? How do you deal with that?

JP: I've tried to keep myself as anonymous as possible, and have not been involved in activism in that area for a while to avoid any perceived conflict. But at the same time, when your research has a political edge, you are an activist of sorts. So, for example, the work I've done around gender diverse or same-sex parenting has connected to this issue of whether the kids raised by same-sex parents are 'all right'. And it's all everyone wants to ask about, '*are the kids all right?*' Over and over again I get asked to write or talk about whether kids with queer parents are damaged compared to other kids. And that is a highly political question. Most people aren't asking if the kids are okay because they really care if the kids *are* okay. Usually it is being asked by people on the ultra-right who want ammunition to vilify gay people, to prove they should not be allowed to have kids. Or, people want a defense against the ultra-right—'*the kids are okay, look the science proves it!*' Really, if they thought the kids were *not* doing well they might be asking what they could do to better support kids who have queer parents, not asking whether or not they should have been born in the first place.

So I hate having to answer the question because it feels like putting up a defence against a question that just shouldn't be asked. It's just that people know these days that they can't directly critique adults' right to be gay, so anti-gay campaigners have to find these other issues to mount their attack—usually they find a way in through the idea they are just protecting children. But I don't think they are protecting anyone. It's also frustrating because generally the evidence we use to debate whether the kids are okay is based on these tiny, little deviations in psychometric measures. I can see why those measures are good in a clinical sense to help individual kids. But are these really a good marker of whether a group of kids is okay? I am not sure. But I am not a psychologist, so maybe not the best person to talk about that. Anyway, all those psychometric measures say the kids are fine, in case there was any doubt.

HD: Does that have an impact on how you do your work or what you put out there? Do you feel constrained by that?

JP: Sometimes. I certainly feel vulnerable because of it at times. When there was controversy over sex education in schools and a lot of academics were being publicly critiqued, everyone felt a bit vulnerable. I took some things down from my blog, laid low. Made sure my personal life was invisible.

But I don't feel constrained as such. I've had lots of thoughts about that sort of tension since you suggested this interview, about how if you're queer and politically engaged and an academic, there's an ongoing tension. But tension is creative as well. Doing the sort of social science research that I do, your job is to unpack what's going on in the world and to question it and to challenge it and imagine what else is possible. That is our job and when you focus on gender and sexuality, it's inherently queer and inherently political in some ways. And so your identity and your job and your politics do converge. And they should. But you constantly have to reflect on your own sense of self and your confidence. You have to be constantly prepared to put yourself out there on all levels—as a researcher and as a writer and personally—and to be rejected and critiqued. It's the whole nature of the game. It's a real confidence trick. But maybe that's what all queer people do—be willing to put ourselves out there because the world looks different to us and we challenge it.

HD: But I can imagine other people who would not perhaps feel the same about confidence as you might. And that is what I'm curious about, whether there is a way in which that queerness, or internalised queer oppression, or women's oppression, sits on you in a particular way that means you're not personally 'Jen who's struggling with her own confidence', but that actually there are structural constraints at play.

JP: Absolutely. And I wouldn't be the first person to say that. I think this game—academia, but the whole world of course—has been designed for cisgender white men, because you do have to be very confident. The people who do really well are those who are very confident in their position, who can talk the talk, who don't question themselves, who haven't had to question themselves. And who's that? Cisgender, straight white men. No disrespect to them. There are plenty of men in that category who do fantastic work and are highly self-reflective. But they just haven't had to question their legitimacy in the world. That's the reality. And, not to mention the time commitment. Once you're a woman with kids it's really very hard to keep up professionally. We all know a lot about that. That's a confidence trick too—it takes confidence just to get up every day, and get everyone out the door and get to work and pretend your day isn't as chaotic as it really is.

HD: So thinking about the family focus of this interview, tell me a bit about your parenting journey.

JP: So I had my first child in 2009. I had another one in 2013. But when I had them I was in two different relationships—a different relationship for each child. So in effect, my children are biological siblings (I carried them both and they have the same donor), but they have two different family experiences because they both have different other parents, other mothers, besides me. But now I live as a single mother and co-parent with their two other mothers. It's complicated. I sometimes feel like I have to draw a picture to explain my family—like a genogram. But for me, that process of having babies and separating and living as a single mother has been an interesting lesson in what it means to be queer.

HD: Tell me more about that lesson in queer.

JP: One thing that surprised me having babies as a lesbian—well there were lots of things that surprised me about having babies—but one thing I don't think I quite expected was that all that stuff around mother guilt … and time pressure, and feeling guilty about going back to work, and trying to make the family perfect and all that. It really did hit me quite hard. I don't know why I thought I would be different. But I thought as a queer parent, maybe I would be a bit liberated from that. Mothers get such a hard time. And what I found was that I felt this enormous pressure to be normal, to be really normal as a mother—*normal* normal. What does that even mean? I have decided it is nostalgia. That nostalgic vision—summer holidays, dad cooking the BBQ, and mum in the kitchen. That ideal upbringing in that very nostalgic way. But I couldn't do it. Once separation and single parenthood was in the mix the nostalgic vision was a mess. It was just a sense of failure.

HD: Do you think that your heterosexual sister would have the same nostalgia—your straight sister would have the same or similar nostalgia about bringing up kids well?

JP: Oh I think she feels the pressure stronger than I do in a way. There is pressure on all women. But she probably focuses on different things, and even not having to have the same gender politics in the household as my sister let me do it from a slightly different angle.

HD: Do you think that there was an added pressure to do a good job because you were a same sex parent?

JP: Yes. And that was really visible to me as a separated parent. There was genuine shame for me in the separation, still is. Like I really struggled with feeling that I was a terrible mother, not being good enough to keep my family together and it was in those moments I really questioned whether there was an extra layer of possible damage for my kids because of being a queer parent. It's crazy though, that sort of shame. There's a sort of intellectual part of me that thinks, '*Get over it, you're allowed to be who you are and the kids are okay*!', and all of that. And I feel a bit silly for naming it as shame. But even when you can intellectually rationalize this sort of shame, it's still a very deep-seated thing. There still really is this pressure deep down, a kind of emotional and social pressure—to be sort of normal, in a way. It's harder to challenge that stuff when there's kids involved—because you have to try to convince yourself that they are ok even when the world tells you that you are not good enough as a parent. It's quite intense. It makes me teary even saying it out loud to be honest.

HD: Can you to talk a little bit more about shame?

JP: Yes. All right. Because no-one does do they?

HD: Because no-one does. And I imagine you're not the only separated lesbian Mum in the world. But I reckon that not many of them are getting to talk about this stuff, which is why I wanted to do this interview, 'The individual is collective' kind of notion. Given that the idea of one mother and a nuclear family is so strong, is there shame for you around having another mother and not another father—not a father, in some way? Or have you gotten over that years ago, just being a lesbian out in the world?

JP: No, no. I think that actually comes back to bite you a bit with kids. Like in some ways I got over that years ago. I've always been pretty out as a lesbian, even when I was young, I didn't struggle much. You know, I lived in a progressive family, I came out in a progressive environment at uni. I had a pretty easy run.

But I would say that awareness of homophobia has hit me more in my older years than in my younger years, some of that—whatever you want to call it—internalised homophobia. Because once you have kids, you're out. You have less choice—you have to be out in all these everyday, mainstream places—the doctor, the school, the childcare, the dentist. And maybe in hindsight I—because I had a ponytail and looked like a straight woman—I passed a lot. I was very acceptable in mainstream life. Mostly I was out. I didn't deliberately pass, but I probably just did. When you have kids and move into the suburbs and you have to go to schools, that, for sure, takes bravery. You don't get to pass and you don't get to choose who you interact with. There's degrees of that, but sometimes you just don't want to be the queer family on the block. You just want to be the normals. Some days, you know? Monday morning, seven AM … you wanna be the normals.

HD: So it feels a bit like there's always someone watching—a spectator in a sense? You're always being witnessed as a queer family?

JP: Maybe, a little bit, yes. You're more visible. It's a bit tiring. But for me too then I've got the layers of separation over that. So I think I've told you that story about going into the administration office at school to enrol my daughter. I had to explain my whole family situation because we were out of the school zone and I needed to justify her attendance. And I just felt awful. So that's when the '*I'm really outside the norm here*' hit home, explaining it to the administration woman at the front office at the school. She was so nice. I was practically in tears and obviously looked upset. She said to me, '*I'll just take it away and get my head around it, shall I?*' But in a nice way, not a derogatory way. The shame was in my head, not coming from her. But it was still real. Not that I live my life in doom and gloom, I think that is important to say. It's just these moments, where difference become more tangible.

HD: So you think separation might feel different for queer parents? Heterosexual people probably feel shame about it too?

JP: I think queer parents have different pressures that aren't often spoken about and that are difficult to speak about. In lesbian families there are two mothers. And there is pressure when it comes to biology and legitimacy. Mothers who are not the birth mother, or biological mother, often feel really vulnerable in the role as a parent—and I reckon this is magnified for some people after separation. If there's insecurities and tensions in the backdrop, that's when it's really going to show or come to the fore. But for me, as a biological mother, I also felt vulnerable as a mother through that process of separating from my partner and found it hard to make sense of this and hard to talk about. I was really conscious of how it might be perceived if I spoke about my grief at being separated from my children or fear of how people might see me. How do I acknowledge that 'biological privilege'—the fact that I don't have to question my legitimacy on those grounds—while still talking about how vulnerable I felt as a mother in that moment? I mean it's all in there but some of it's unspeakable.

But when I think about it, perhaps it is not just about biology. There is such as lack of cultural imagination for two mothers—even more so for two fathers. Because culturally, there's one mother. Every vision of motherhood, there is *just one mother*. Even though the lesbian community has done a massive amount to shift that and to queer that vision of what a family looks like, most of the world doesn't understand how two mother families operate and it can be hard to write that script for yourself—especially in separation. You sometimes step on each other's toes a bit to feel legitimate or safe as a mother—in my experience anyway, a bit of two-mother turf-war. It can feel vulnerable.

HD: Yes. So two-mother turf-war …

JP: Sort of. Like you both … you grow up with this idea of what it means to be a mother. And then you have to share that role. It can be quite confronting. It can be amazing when it works well. But obviously people separate for a reason and it isn't always working well. So you have to learn to reimagine motherhood in a two-mother family in quite interesting ways—and I am still doing that as a single mother. It's kinda ironic.

HD: You also talked about the absence of imagination. And I guess that's what you're talking about now, is that a cultural imagining of what family is?

JP: Well you really do have to craft that when your family is different. Same-sex couple families have to craft that and, bloody hell, you have to craft and recraft when you are a separated same-sex couple family. There is no cultural scripting for that. But maybe there is liberation in that too. But that's not always easy. Coming back to that issue of whether the kids are okay, I had this weird time where I was writing about whether kids are okay and presenting evidence that shows that kids are okay in same-sex families, but kids who experience their parents' divorce or kids with single parents are much more vulnerable. It felt really weird writing that. So at the same time as I'm sort of feeling like I could be critiqued for being a queer parent with a political agenda, justifying why the kids are okay, what I'm writing is that my kids might not be okay.

HD: Yes. Wow that must be tough.

JP: Yes it sucks. It sucks. And no-one knows that. No-one—because my story's so hidden, no-one sees that, obviously, because I am just presenting evidence in a fairly objective framework.

HD: So when you're writing 'the kids are okay', you've got another narrative going in your head that says that 'mine are not okay'?

JP: Well yes and no. I think this is where the queer stuff comes in. People assume kids do best in a heterosexual, nuclear family. Every other family form has to justify itself. So our basis for measuring 'okay' is flawed, because there are plenty of kids raised in stable, hetero families who aren't okay. We just don't look at them as a group.

Also what do you really mean by okay? What if your kid is emotionally up and down, but highly creative and a wonderful artist. Are they not okay? What if a kid has a tough childhood, but develops into a highly resilient adult? Was their life okay? I am not entirely sure I know the answer to that. I just know that we need to always question the assumptions made in all this stuff.

And I reckon queer people are good at questioning this stuff. We have had to. We know that most assumptions people make in the world don't make sense. We live with that. And so for me in a way, being queer, or living a queer life, is just as simple as actually trying to challenge some of those assumptions and some of that shame—honestly—around divorce and separation and single parenting and normal parenting and what makes kids okay. And shame seems really like an intense word I think because there's such a long history now of divorce and separation and single parenting, but I think it's still really there for women in particular, or men probably too. The sense of failure and that families are meant to be a certain way and parents are meant to be a certain way and you're meant to raise your kids in a certain way. It's very strong.

HD: Because there's a queer lens that sits over that and makes it harsher at this moment in history?

JP: No, I think the queer lens is forgiving, at least for me. Because it's a lens that sort of reminds me you can—you're allowed to lead your life differently and that actually for generations of us there's creativity and resilience in being queer and celebrating not being normal. And why would my kids be any different? So they may not have had the normal, heterosexual or even homonormative life. But that doesn't mean that that's a lesser life. It's still a cool life. And that's a queer narrative I think.

And that's a narrative I get to hold onto as a queer woman, rather than being imbued in the normative heterosexual frame. That's really important to me. The experience of queer for me now is as a separated, single parent. And recognizing that a different family is okay and it can be fun and subversive in a great way and not a failure is like a queer project of sorts. And that's where queers come from, you know? We're not pathology and we're not aberrations and we're not doing the wrong thing. We're living our lives differently to this normative standard. And there's real strength and pride in that. And community. So yes, that's what queer is for me now. I'm not cool and I am not particularly radical in my everyday life. I am kinda middle-aged. I am just figuring out how to be okay as a parent.

HD: How does Marriage Equality sit over all of this for you, just thinking about the temperature of gay activism at the moment, of queer life?

JP: Oh I felt really alienated from it, partly because of all of this. Partly because for me I felt so alienated from the homo-nuclear family model. And alienated from some of that politics which was a bit geared toward 'please like me'. '*Please like us because we are normal and we want to be married and monogamous and have kids just like you*'. The stupid vote forced us all into that position. And I didn't feel like I wanted to be that. And I certainly didn't feel like I was that or could be that. I am not against marriage equality at all. I think it's cool. I just felt very detached from the whole thing. I think a lot of people did.

HD: *In your book,* Movement, Knowledge and Motion: Gay Activism and HIV AIDS in Australia*—you said, 'Vigilance is necessary to ensure that once the basics have been achieved, the cause does not get forgotten.' Is there any way you can apply this statement to activism around queer parenting and families. While there's a lot that's been achieved, do you think there's a sort of greater cause that needs to be held onto around family activism and queer family?*

JP: I think there's a greater cause that needs to be held onto around diversity, and that family diversity doesn't get lost. So I think the world will come to grips with gay marriage and kids of same sex couples. But there's much broader diversity than that. Trans people who transition after they've had kids, or before, or trans men who are pregnant. Even queer single parents. There's lots of us out there. The narrative that kids can't adapt to their parents changing, separating, living their lives and being human and being gender diverse or diverse in other ways needs to be challenged. I think it's important that that keeps getting challenged without it seeming like we aren't doing the best we can for our kids. I'm not a child psychologist so I don't want to be attacked for not taking kids concerns seriously. I know change and loss is tough for kids and they need support. But I am not convinced that kids can't thrive despite this. And we need to talk about that. Why can't we celebrate family diversity in all its glory?

With Marriage Equality too, lots of people have said this, what does it mean for diversity in terms of sexuality and relationship styles and status and people who aren't monogamous and people who are polyamorous and people who are single and have casual sex or are just queer in other ways? I think that's been dropped off, that celebration of diversity is what needs to be protected. Queer community used to do this so well. Celebrate diversity. It used to be the cause more overtly, before marriage equality came along.

And also, not sanitizing things so much. There is bodies and there's sex and there's pleasure. And sex and sexuality is important in a lot of queer culture, queers know how to have fun and how to do sex. And a lot of that was erased I think from the Love is Love campaign. We talked about relationships and romance, but not sex. I think there's this pressure to sanitise it all a bit. But why should we? Sex, sexuality, pleasure. It's part of diversity. And maybe that sort of links back to the queer family thing too. For me, queer the narrative, even though it adds a layer of shame or whatever sometimes, it also adds a layer of *'fuck, it's okay to do life differently!'* It's cool and there's joy and pleasure in that and liberation.

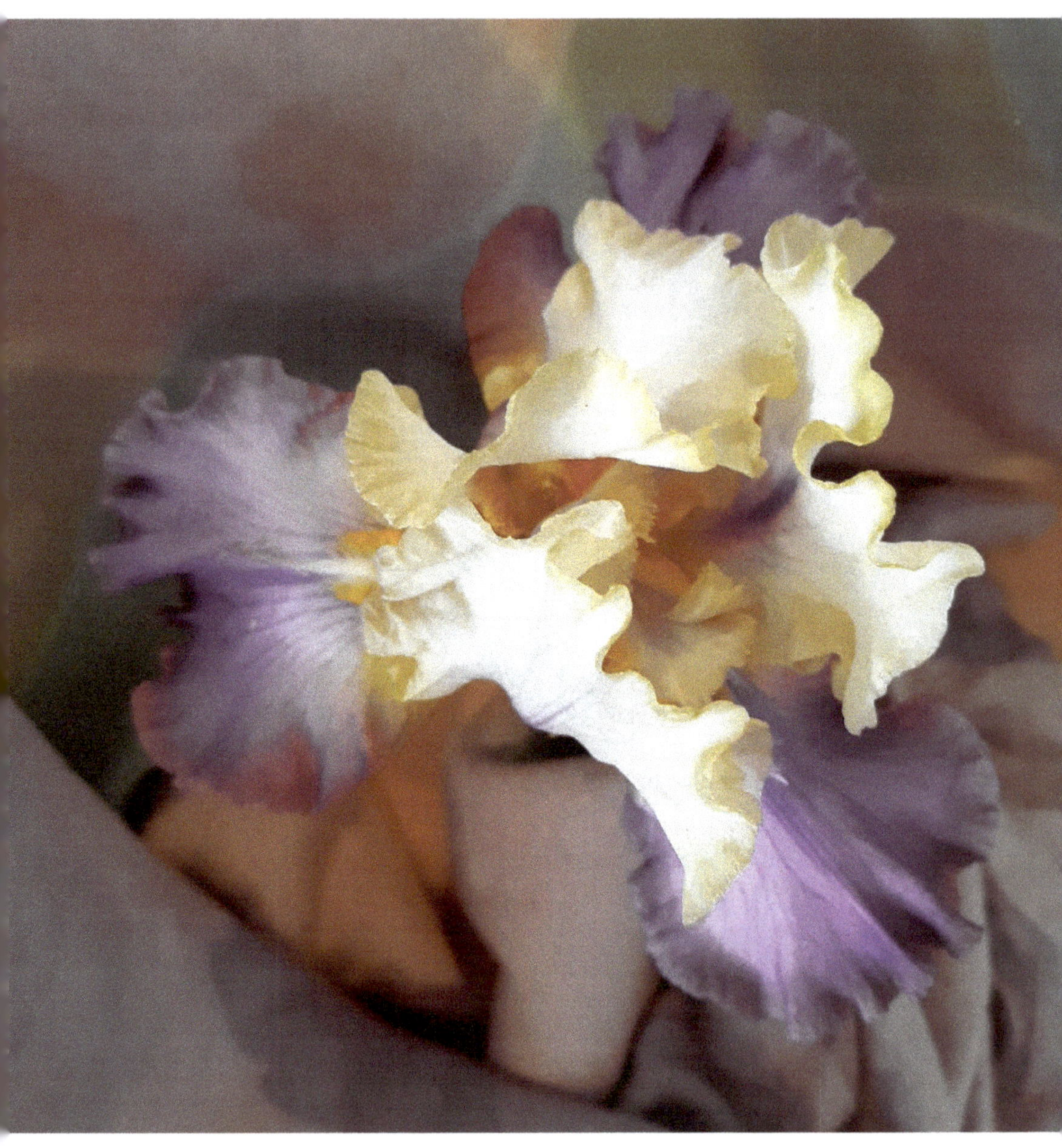

HENRY VON DOUSSA | IRIS 2

ESSAYS
TALKS
POSTS

Dean Smith

Together – A Senator's Perspective

From the Pride WA 2018 Program

In the United States, 'Log Cabin Republicans' are a group of LGBT Republicans and straight allies who honour the legacy of Abraham Lincoln, through their support for equality under the law, free markets, individual liberty, limited government, and a strong national defence.

The name is said to originate from the suggestion that Lincoln founded the Republican Party on the philosophies of individual liberty and equality under the law for all.

When reflecting on 'Together', it's worth remembering the immortal quote of Abraham Lincoln, delivered on the 16th of June 1858, when fighting another form of inequality in American society, that 'A house divided against itself cannot stand'.

More than at any other time in Pride WA's history, this year presents us with the most powerful of opportunities, and we should reflect on the very real and meaningful success we have achieved by acting 'Together'.

The legislative change to enact marriage equality, putting an end to discrimination against LGBTIQ people is living proof of the success we can achieve when working 'Together' with friends, families and allies.

'Together' is about acting and speaking as one.

But 'Together' doesn't have to mean we have to sacrifice our individuality or diversity.

'Together' recognises the values we share in common are greater than those that divide—it respects the difference that is so cleverly captured in the phrase 'same, same but different'.

And what are these things common to all of us? —The pursuit of a guarantee that everyone's rights are protected under the law; the desire to be treated with dignity and respect by our families, our neighbours, colleagues and by strangers; and the freedom to be true to ourselves and live life on our terms, freely and openly, and in a manner that is authentic to us.

Together, Pride WA, and every LGBTIQ Western Australian can stand proud.

'Together' also requires vigilance, because the achievements won through years of campaigning can all too easily be eroded and lost.

For the moment, these are concerns for another day.

It's time to celebrate the things that brought us together, the values that keep us bound, and set out our sights on a brighter future, 'Together'.

SENATOR DEAN SMITH
Senator for Western Australia

Alison Thorne

Remembering the Pink Triangle

A call for rainbow atheists to resist the far right!

Presented by Alison Thorne on 30 October 2018 at an event hosted by Rainbow Atheists.

I'd like to start by acknowledging that we meet this evening on the stolen lands of the Kulin Nation. I pay my respects to elders and pledge my solidarity, not only to elders, but also to the young warriors in the struggle. I'd especially like to acknowledge inspiring First Nations elders from the LGBTIQ community such as local legend, Noel Tovey; Tiwi Island sista girl, Crystal Johnson; and feisty lesbian activist, Esther Montgomery who is a Mardudhunera woman from the Pilbara.

A hearty thanks to Rainbow Atheists for organising this very timely gathering. With 'religious freedom' becoming the latest manufactured cause that right-wing forces, both inside and outside parliament, are organising around, there's never been a better time to explore the lessons of history and to talk about what is needed to defeat the emboldened conservative, right-wing populist and outright fascist forces that are seeking to extend their influence and win recruits to their menacing agenda.

In this talk, I'll be speaking about the far right in general—some openly fascist and some not. A grouping or political party is openly fascist when it is seeking to build a violent mass movement of the disaffected based to stopping workers and the oppressed from organising.

I thought it might be useful to share the basis of my rainbow atheism. My working-class family is from Yorkshire in England. We migrated to Australia as '10-pound poms' when I was six years old. My childhood was mostly secular, although my family were nominally Church of England and would have ticked that box on the census. I began identifying as an atheist after I became a Marxist feminist. I embraced gay liberation in my late teens and threw myself into the movement, which in the late '70s was awash with exciting ideas about what was needed to win our freedom.

My quest to understand the basis of homosexual oppression quickly led me to the discovery that before the rise of private property, society was matriarchal and communal, gender identity was fluid and sexuality was free. This changed gradually over generations with the rise of private property. The new economic order required its own institutions: women were enslaved in strict male-headed households comprised initially of wives, children and slaves. Religious taboos were imposed to repress residual sexual and gender diversity.

Wow, what an epiphany—the institutions that oppressed my youthful self and all my friends—the law, the church, and the stiflingly oppressive institution of the monogamous, patriarchal, heterosexual family—hadn't always existed, and they arose alongside private property to serve the ruling class!

*

It was in the early 80s, that I also first encountered two socialist feminist organisations—the Freedom Socialist Party and sister organisation, Radical Women. I was impressed by their pioneering work, including a series of articles published in the *Freedom Socialist* newspaper in the late 70s called *Gay Resistance the Hidden History.* This series, which was later published as a booklet, documents the Judeo-Christian taboo against homosexuality, describing how Jewish and then Christian religion 'associated free sexuality with the Great Mother cults of the ancient matrilineal world, and used sexual prohibitions as a weapon against the lingering, embedded influence of matriarchal customs among the people.'

The Christians, then, 'borrowed the Judaic taboo against sexual freedom and homoerotic behaviour and proceeded to extend the taboo against virtually all sexual enjoyment to a scope undreamed of by even the Hebrew patriarchs.' The pamphlet then describes what it characterises as a 'medieval holocaust' against women's self-determination and free sexual expression, condemning all sexual activity occurring outside the sacrament of heterosexual marriage.

Once I understood the basis of my own oppression as a worker and a woman who was not heterosexual, I could not un-know what I had learnt. I joined both the Freedom Socialist Party and Radical Women in 1982 and commenced an action-packed life as a Marxist feminist. This philosophy informs every aspect of my world view. I have a scientific materialist approach to the world, appreciating that the physical world ***precedes*** the world of ideas. I came to understand that not only Christianity, but also all religious doctrines, are idealist philosophies. So, for the last four decades I have been ticking 'Atheist' on my census, which is just about the only time in predominantly secular Australia I am even asked the question.

*

I have titled this talk, 'Remembering the Pink Triangle: A call for rainbow atheists to resist the far right,' because I firmly believe in the importance of studying history and then applying the lessons. When we remember the pink triangle, we think first of oppression: of the chilling horror of the Nazis making homosexuals one of their scapegoats as they came to power in Germany, snuffing out all democratic rights and imposing more than 12 years of fascist rule.

But we also think of struggle as the gay liberation movement in the 70s reclaimed the pink triangle and turned it into a symbol of queer resistance! We are reminded of how the AIDS Coalition to Unleash Power (ACT-UP) adopted the inverted pink triangle along with the powerful call to arms that 'silence equals death.' While gay liberationists were marching on the streets with the Tshirts, badges, placards and banners proudly displaying the pink triangle, the movement was also part of the sweeping struggles taking place that won queer studies on campuses alongside women's studies, Aboriginal and labour history and ethnic studies. The outpouring of writing resulted in published history that ceased describing the past from the perspective of the winners. Voices other than rich, white, heterosexual men became heard!

There was a flowering of historical discovery: evidence was re-examined and important stories painstakingly uncovered. Those who survived were inspired to tell their stories. Important memoires such as Heinz Heger's *The Men with the Pink Triangle* packed a powerful punch. Alongside the truth telling the horrors, a huge amount of invaluable historical work asked how and why did fascism come to power and crucially, could it have been stopped?

*

Studying the decades before fascism is rich with lessons. The first homosexual rights organisation in the world emerged in Germany at the end of the 19th century. For more than three decades, the Scientific Humanitarian Committee, led by Dr Magnus Hirschfield, was a key part of a large queer community with a thriving hub based in Berlin. The committee educated around sexuality, organised for homosexual rights and campaigned to repeal paragraph 175 of the German Penal Code. They gathered more than 6,000 signatures on a petition demanding the repeal of this anti-gay clause, with support coming from prominent community leaders. This organising became part of a struggle for sexual reform across Europe. The pinnacle of its success was the Bolsheviks' removal of all laws restricting consensual sexual conduct, just two months after the October Russian Revolution. They also legalised divorce and abortion.

All this took place in a broader ***political*** context. Socialist ideas were growing in popularity, with the German Social Democratic workers' party attracting huge numbers of members. First-wave feminism was sweeping Europe. Germany was no exception, where the movement was demanding civil rights, reproductive justice and equal education. Workers were demanding healthier living conditions in the cities, and a radical youth movement attracted thousands. This also took place in a broader ***economic*** context. During the 1920s, the German economy was saddled with the legacy of debilitating reparations and loss of territory from the First World War. This posed significant costs, especially on heavy industry.

Ordinary people experienced unemployment, shortages and inflation. Heavy industry, keen to shore up profits, cranked out goods but, with the population squeezed, much of this production failed to find a market. Then, in the late 20s a global financial crisis hit the already beleaguered German economy.

Fascism becomes an option for the capitalists during times of economic crisis. The big end of town needs to squeeze workers harder to make more profits. But if the movements are well organised, they'll resist. Faced with this situation, scapegoats come in handy to distract people from the real source of their misery. Using this approach, the far right will seek to build its own mass fascist movement. This is exactly what happened in Germany.

At first the fascist threat was small, it could have been easily stopped if all of fascism's targets had united to stop them building a mass movement of street thugs. But this did not happen in Germany because of disastrous political errors.

While the German working class and the movements for social change were well organised, they supported two mass parties—the Social Democratic Party and the Communist Party. Tragically, *the socialists believed that the constitution and the capitalist state would keep them safe* from the Nazi menace, while the Communist Party made a different, but just as fatal, mistake. Stalinism dominated the communist movement and *assumed there was little difference between the Nazis and the socialists, who they called social fascists.* The communists also *failed to recognise the seriousness of the situation and refused to form a united front* with the socialists.

To learn more about this period of history, I highly recommend a collection of writing by Trotsky, published as the *Struggle Against Fascism in Germany.* Trotsky, by this time in exile and living on the run from the forces of Stalinism, had a small core of supporters who argued the urgency of the socialist and communist parties working together to defeat the fascists through a united front of all who fascists seek to target. By the time those in leadership woke up and understood that the goal of fascism is to crush working class organising and all mass movements independent of the fascist state, to put women's reproduction under Nazi control and to snuff out democratic rights entirely, it was too late. Fascism had arrived. That fascism in Germany resulted in a holocaust against Jews, Roma people, trade unionists, communists, homosexuals and people with disabilities is now well known. Less well known is that: *with the right strategy, it could have been stopped.*

*

So, what of today? We are living and organising in an increasingly polarised world. The results are deadly, particularly for people of colour, including LGBTIQ people. Far-right parties of both fascist and right-wing populist varieties are on the rise across Europe: we see this with Golden Dawn in Greece, the Sweden Democrats, the National Front in France, AfD (Alternative for Germany), the Freedom Party in Austria and Jobbik in Hungary. Last year, white supremacists from across the U.S. marched in Charlottesville in a Unite the Right Rally where one rammed his car into a crowd of counter-protesters, killing one and injuring 19. Just this week we've seen Robert Bowers—a far-right, anti-Semitic, anti-immigrant man—perpetrate a mass shooting that killed 11 people in a synagogue in Pittsburgh.

Indonesia is in the grip of right-wing populism with hard-line Islamist groups and the conservative politicians who back them, ramping up homophobia and transphobia. The repression is forcing people underground and leading to a rise in HIV infections, because people are too scared to access services. In Brazil, Bolsonaro, an ultra-right candidate backed by the military, recently won the presidential race. Bolsonaro has a far-right agenda, which includes extreme homophobia. He infamously said, '*I would not be incapable of loving a gay son. I prefer that he die in an accident*'. This is happening in a country that is one of the most dangerous places in the world to be an LGBTIQ person, with homophobic crimes, including murders, reaching epidemic proportions. *Transwomen in Brazil have a life expectancy of just 35 years!*

This is the global context, whilst here in Australia we also have a fight on our hands. Conservatives, right-wing populists and open neo-Nazis are also organising in Australia. They are organising on the streets, aiming to build a mass movement. Since early 2015, when 'Reclaim Australia' held rallies around the country, including one in Melbourne's Federation Square, there's been provocation after provocation through far-right and Nazi actions. There's also been a parade of fascists, 'alt-right' and other assorted nasties visiting, from Milo Yiannopolous to Lauren Southern to Nigel Farage. Meanwhile, the government stopped Chelsea Manning from visiting Australia on so-called character grounds!

Fascists paid a visit to community radio station 3CR and to the Melbourne Anarchist Club. They invaded and harassed local council meetings in the City of Yarra and Moreland after these councils spoke out against celebrating Australia Day. They've also disrupted rallies and harassed participants, including actions in solidarity with the Palestinian people and refugee rights. In parliament, the right wing prevented marriage equality from being legislated long after it was well established that there was mass community support. And they succeeded in imposing the odious postal survey, which inflicted such pain on the LGBTIQ community. They've gutted the Safe Schools Program. And just this month we've seen One Nation propose a motion to denounce 'anti-white racism', based on the white supremacist slogan 'It's OK to be white'. This initially got the backing of the Liberal Party, until they realised it wouldn't play well in the Wentworth by-election.

*

The far right in Australia is globally connected and takes up the same causes. They'll tap into any issue they think may help them build their movement. We have flag waving nationalism through to admiration for Donald Trump. They defend Australia Day, while fascists recently defaced a monument to the stolen generation. They want only the 'right kind' of immigrants, generating outpourings of support for white South African farmers, while fuelling Islamophobic fear-mongering over everything from Halal food to mosques and schools. They hate feminism. They 'march for the babies,' champion men's rights and oppose the Family Court as biased in favour of women.

They lampoon political correctness as a tool to silence ordinary folk, while selectively championing free speech to spread their poison. They demand increased law-and-order measures and use xenophobia to fuel insecurity as the economy unravels. Their hysterical policing of the gender binary knows no bounds! The latest cause celebre of the right wing is so-called 'religious freedom.' Once again, this internationally connected movement is taking its cue from battles overseas, such as the U.S. wedding cake battle. The Ruddock Review into religious freedom became a weapon for the Right to bash the LGBTIQ community, which would force limitations on the marriage equality victory. It received more than 16,500 submissions, many equating religious freedom with the right to discriminate. The task of the movement now is to get organised and make sure this tactic backfires, and does so spectacularly!

The religious exemptions to anti-discrimination protections have existed for years. While some LGBTIQ activists and feminists as well as the Independent Education Union have continued to speak out against this travesty, it was not widely known until recently. The combination of the Ruddock Review, coupled with the LGBTIQ movement finally moving on from its almost single-issue focus on marriage equality, means that this issue is now getting traction. There's real potential ***now*** to build on the public support, demonstrated by the marriage win, to get these odious exemptions scrapped.

LGBTIQ teachers in religious schools live in fear of being outed, causing immense stress. These exemptions are currently being used. In 2006, a divorced principal was sacked from a Catholic school for remarrying, and in 2012 a pregnant teacher was sacked from a Christian school for being unmarried. This fight needs to link the LGBTIQ and feminist movements as well as the trade union movement.

As a socialist, I do not oppose the right of people to hold religious beliefs. The state has absolutely no business interfering. Everyone has the right to profess whatever religion they choose, and this includes the right to have no religion. A key issue with the religious exemptions is that *religious schools in Australia are publicly funded institutions*. As we campaign for the full repeal of all religious exemptions, we should also be educating about the need for the separation of church and state. Religious influence must be removed from all public institutions, and the state must immediately stop funding *all* religious organisations!

*

This talk is a call for Rainbow Atheists to fire up and resist the far right. First and foremost, everyone who is concerned about these issues needs get active—resisting the far right is not something that can be delegated to someone else. We *all* have a role in it. We're also vastly more effective when we join an organisation that shares our perspective, so that we can campaign collectively. This boosts our efforts! It would be great to see Rainbow Atheists move from being a Facebook group into being an activist group—there's certainly no shortage of things to do.

For those interested in finding out more about socialist feminism, check out the Freedom Socialist Party, starting with our publications the *Freedom Socialist* and *Freedom Socialist Organiser*. We welcome those who would like to know more to join one of our study groups, to work with us in the movements and, if you agree, we'd invite you to join. We also need to absorb those lessons from German history and apply them to Australia today. Neo-Nazis are organising and they cannot be ignored or simply dismissed as a joke. Those like the Freedom Socialist Party and Radical Women, who have been countering fascist grouplets, have kept them small. But they are not defeated, and they are just looking for that spark to build a mass fascist movement.

We're working as part of a group called PUSH! Organising and Educating to Build a United Front against Fascism. PUSH is a nucleus seeking to build a united front of all of fascism's targets that is democratic, disciplined, accountable and effective. It would be great to have Rainbow Atheists come on board. Check out the PUSH call to action and get in touch to become involved. History tells us that there is way too much at stake. Don't sit on the sidelines—the time to get active is now!

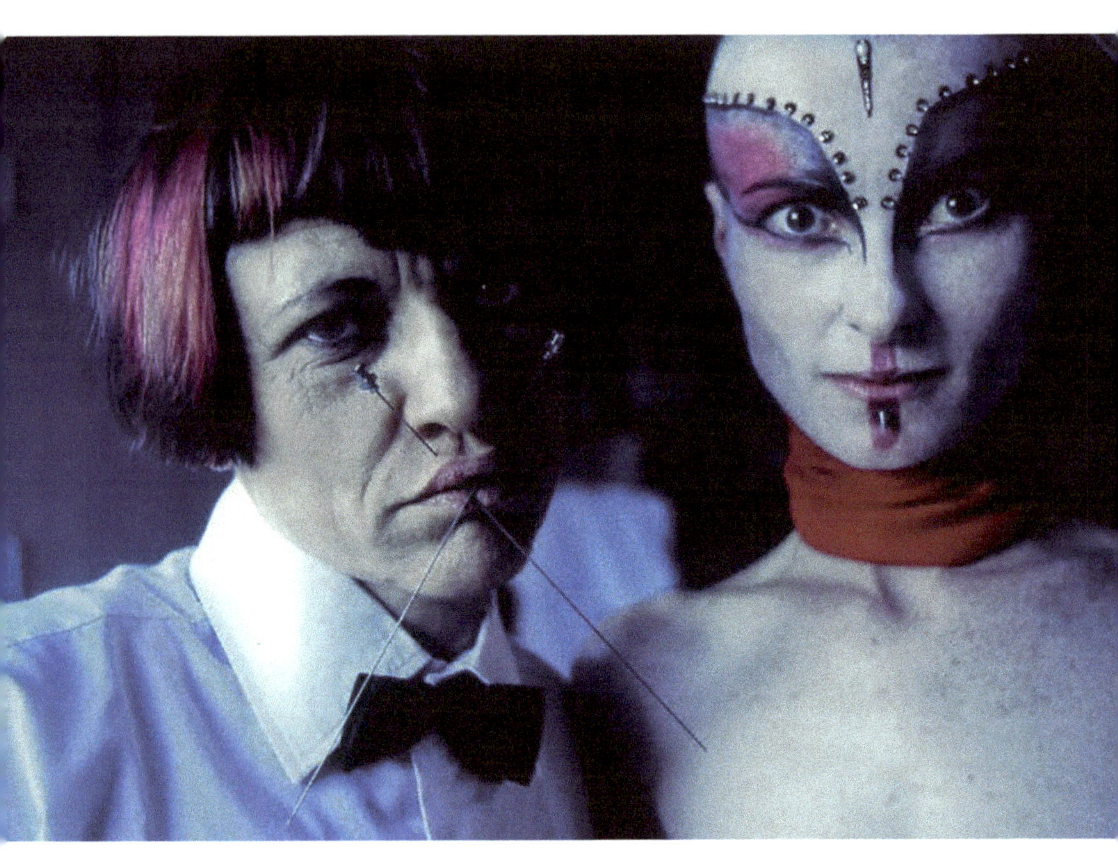

JAMIE JAMES | senVoodoo, Specimen, Body Art, Australian Museum, 2000

fleshnest

insect eyed I find you first find jewel bug
cuckoo wasp flower chafer
bright open dark down
lucent even inside

city light gifts pushes paints a second set of pupils or
white holes punching through irises
what can these eyes diffract

convex the lens finds intervals tries to flip the flicker
strip to draw down derivatives to uncurve a cell
count of billions to turn into a bowl a cupped hand
a sickle a slick slip from ledge to ledge

follow fingerwidth carmine a silver arrow
trace hold tighten a red throat
left to black tie high collar
are you cold in all that blue

pinned there are more ways to speak than any of us
remember did I say writing is dancing is butterfly
wings crushed velvet a compound eye

insect splayed I find a fourth eye dark in the bend
of light trace the touchline
wriggle through the mouthgate the smallest hole
make a fleshnest wrap wet wings around the fall

QUINN EADES

Rebecca Ryall

Queering the classroom: an examination of heteronormativity and cisnormativity in the Catholic school context

Introduction

Education in Australia is both a right and a legally regulated expectation. In addition to academic instruction, schools play an important role in socialising children toward adult norms. Through the physical spaces of the classroom and the playground, and the virtual spaces of various curricula, schools represent important cultural sites for the production of citizens. If the social and political climate of the school is 'not supportive of every child, then true educational experiences do not exist' (Meyer 2010, p. 10). Australian research reveals that 'compared to cisgendered young people, transgender and gender diverse students were significantly more likely to have…suffered discriminatory physical abuse…to self-harm and attempt suicide' (Jones & Hillier 2013, p. 287). This paper uses a queer approach to examine aspects of the educational experience available at a local Catholic high school. It aims to illuminate the hegemonic cultural identities and relations of power, using educational resources and research from the fields of feminist family studies, queer theory and pedagogy, and cultural studies.

Queer, heteronormativity & cisnormativity

Deconstruction of heteronormativity and cisnormativity illuminates the power of the school—as a cultural and social institution—to regulate and reinforce gender categories. The representative school is an independent religious institution shaped by the values and traditions of the Marist Brothers and the Presentation Sisters. The mission statement of the school is to 'enable students to achieve the fullness of life' and the motto is 'In word and deed'. The school possesses a comprehensive safe school and bullying policy (drawn from the National Safe Schools Framework) which sets a clear intention to protect the following student rights: 'the right to feel safe and comfortable and for property to be safe; the right to travel to and from school feeling safe; the right to be treated with courtesy and respect, and the right to learn'. School governance is overseen by various committees comprising both Marist Brothers and members of the laity. The school is bound by Federal and State Government directions in delivery of curriculum. The *Melbourne Declaration on Educational Goals for Young Australians* 'articulates nationally consistent future directions and aspirations for Australian schooling agreed to by all Australian Education Ministers' (ACARA 2009). This nationally endorsed policy document obliges all school sectors to provide a quality education, free from discrimination based on the grounds of gender and sexual orientation (among others). It is important to note however that religious organisations and institutions in Australia are currently exempt from Federal and State anti-discrimination legislation (Sex Discrimination Amendment: Sexual Orientation, Gender Identity and Intersex Status Act, 2013).

Heteronormativity has been extensively interrogated by theorists and practitioners within the fields of education, family and feminist studies. Heteronormativity is conceptualised as an ideological composite that fuses together biological sex, gender identity and expression, sexuality and family constellations into a singular theoretical complex. Essentially, distinct binary oppositions—male/female, masculine/feminine, heterosexual/non heterosexual and normal family/deviant family—are conflated, and heteronormativity becomes the unexamined and unopposed gateway to power, rights and resources. Scholars of gender and sexuality, and queer theorists (Butler 1990; Connell 1995; Sullivan 2003), have effectively argued that the categories of gender, biological sex and sexual orientation represent three distinct aspects of a human being's character and identity, although intersectionalities do exist. Scholars in crip theory (McRuer 2006) would add that heteronormativity also implies able-bodiedness, and those interested in race and whiteness studies (Durie, 2003; Moreton-Robinson, 2006) would argue that whiteness is an implied aspect of heteronormativity.

Cisnormativity can be understood as an invisible ideological framework which privileges those individuals whose gender identification matches their assigned birth gender. The unexamined dominance of cisgendered hegemonic discourse establishes and reinforces relations of power in which some voices are heard, and others are not. Figure 1 illustrates the informational and institutional erasure, or silencing, of the voices and experiences of gender diverse individuals in the institutional context.

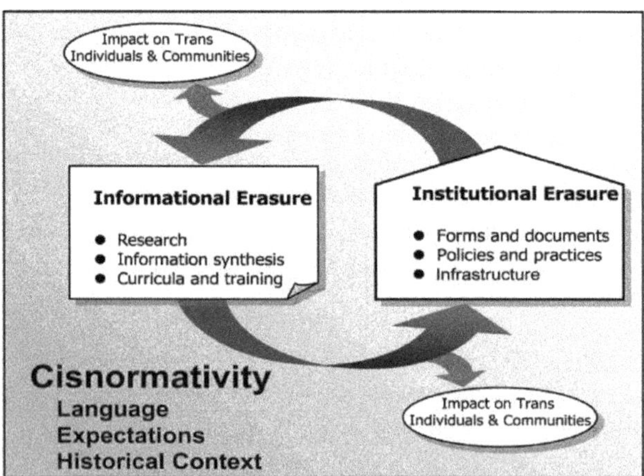

Figure 1: Cisnormativity in an institutional context (Bauer, G et al. 2009, p. 356).

Queer theorists are concerned with problematising and deconstructing the concept of 'normality'. Warner positions queer as 'that which opposes not just the normal behaviour of the social, but the *idea* of normal behaviour' (Warner 1993, p. xxvii). Through deconstruction of notions of deviance and normativity, and analysis of cultural and discursive practices which create identities, it becomes possible to reinscribe categories of gender and sexuality. This repositioning affords an understanding of the way that institutions, policies and practices impact those who have the least power.

Deconstructing the school: governance

The complex system of governance of any school apportions power, of varying degrees, across myriad domains. Being a federally funded school brings expectations for any educational institution. Having a religious basis brings another layer of complexity, with religious institutions bound by the expectations of their own governing bodies. The classroom environment is governed by the specific teacher, with their own pedagogy, ideology and socially constructed prejudices. Within the classroom, and the social milieu of the playground, 'the institutional gaze is distributed and re-distributed' (Foucault 1977, p. 173) from the hierarchy and 'throughout internal mechanisms…the individual begins to take responsibility for regulating their own behaviour and that of others' (Cumming-Potvin & Martino 2018, p. 41). The students themselves become complicit in the construction and regulation of hegemonic heteronormativity.

Conditions of entry: enrolment & uniform

The representative school examined in this paper is positioned as one of the best performing high schools in the local area, in terms of academic success and sporting prowess. The school offers places to about 1500 students across years seven to twelve and regularly maintains waiting lists for places. In examination of heteronormativity and cisnormativity in this context, enrolment forms were analysed for their construction or regulation of hegemonic normativity. Enrolment forms gather personal information about both the prospective student, and their family/ies. Following requests for full name and date of birth, prospective students are asked their 'gender', with the provision of space for the applicant to nominate 'M' or 'F'. References to parents are not gender specific (parent/carer is used in data collection) and the form allows nomination of three parent/carers but only allows space for two parent/carers who live with the child. Requiring prospective students to nominate their gender as either male or female conflates biological sex with gender and fails to recognise and collect data relating to gender diversity. Information collected at enrolment is not useful in understanding diversity in family arrangements.

As with most private schools, students are expected to adhere to a strict uniform code, with punitive consequences for non-adherents, whether they be on school grounds or other public or private property. The Uniform guidelines (available on the College website) clearly define the College's expectations regarding wearing of the uniform, providing a 'boy's uniform' option and a 'girl's uniform' option. The NSW Department of Education School Uniform Policy (NSW Department of Education 2018) requires schools to offer uniform options which: 'promote a sense of belonging for students; take into account the diverse nature of the student population and comply with anti-discrimination legislation'. This policy was amended in June 2018 to require that all female students have access to a shorts or pants option. Additionally, the NSW Department of Education Legal Issues Bulletin No. 55 (NSW Department of Education 2014), outlines the rights and responsibilities of schools with respect to transgender identifying students, with particular reference to access to alternate gender markers, access to uniform of their chosen gender, and access to appropriate bathroom and toilet facilities. Again, being a religious organisation, the school is exempt from compliance with anti-discrimination legislation. Being an independent school, the school is also under no obligation to meet the requirements imposed by the NSW Department of Education.

The representative school is a co-educational facility whose demographic is composed of 45% identifying as male and 55% identifying as female. As data collection only allows for students to identify as male or female, it is not possible to know what percentage of the student cohort identifies as gender diverse. Additionally, no data is reported which identifies the prevalence of non-standard family relationships, such as same sex parents, or relationships including gender diverse individuals or polyamorous relationships. Enrolment forms do identify single parent families, and also collect information about multiple carers, but this information does not appear in the College's Annual Report and therefore is probably not instructive in development of policy or delivery of content. The National Safe Schools Framework reports that 10% of school students are same sex attracted (Mitchell et al 2014), 4% of students identify as either transgender or gender diverse (Clark et al 2013) and 1.7% of students are intersex (Blackless et al 2000). If these statistics were to hold true within the context of the representative school, it would be reasonable to expect that about 150 of their current student cohort are same sex attracted, about 60 identify as transgender or gender diverse, and roughly 25 intersex students attend the school. Homosexuality, gender non-conformity and intersex status are not religiously mediated, so it is reasonable to assume that, although this is a religious institution, the diversity of the student population will reflect the diversity of broader society. Without appropriate data collection, however, it is not possible to know with any certainty. This is reflective of the informational and institutional erasure referred to in Figure 1.

Classroom discourse

Given that high school children spend around five hours of each school day in a classroom, the discourse of the classroom requires scrutiny. Classroom discourse is 'any type of discourse which goes on in the classroom: between teacher and students, or among students with or without the teacher' (Pontecorva 1997, p. 169). Cumming-Potvin and Martino (2018) gathered information from West Australian secondary English teachers as to their willingness and ability to set texts of their choosing, for discussion and analysis. They noted that while a small number of respondents did set texts in which a leading character displayed diversity of sexuality or gender, these characters were invariably troubled or cast as victims. While diversity in texts is to be applauded, displaying characters thus perpetuates the narrative of marginalization and social isolation of the gender or sexually diverse student. This research illuminates the pervasive discomfort experienced by many teachers when confronted with issues they view as controversial. Meyer (2010) examines the 'hidden curriculum', shaped by informal jokes and comments between and among students and staff, evidenced by school-sanctioned events, and the sporting and other activities valued by the school community (p. 61). This 'hidden curriculum' subtly informs both the information that is delivered, and how it is delivered to students, and more crucially, what conversations are not conducted.

The religious context does on the surface seem to introduce levels of complexity, but scholars are divided as to the appropriate response of the religious community to students whose identities fall outside of the heterosexual matrix. In his examination of queer theology, Henry calls for an 'educational commitment that embraces the spiritual identity of the young person in the educational encounter that it offers, while also refusing to script what that identity ought to be as a consequence of this encounter' (2018, p. 14). Edmund Rice Education Australia—a network of Catholic schools—has developed a policy document guiding educators and school leaders in the provision of an education which is inclusive and committed to justice and solidarity (Edmund Rice Education Australia 2017). This document directly links inclusion with the Catholic mission of education and recommends schools revisit and revise all bullying and discrimination policy, with explicit attention to acknowledging the presence of students with diverse sexuality and gender, and protecting the rights and dignity of these students.

Students at the representative school are routinely separated into gendered groups for sporting activities, sexual health education, and the healthy relationships program 'Boys of Honour, Girls with Grace' (worthy of discussion in a standalone paper, in the opinion of this writer). Additionally, bathrooms remain gendered, with only five 'accessible' or unisex bathrooms to accommodate 1500 students across two campuses. Every time a student needs to use the toilet or is required to join a gendered group for sport or class activities, the student is required to announce or affirm their gender and given only two options. Not only does this silence and isolate the voices of students of diverse gender, it also serves to further entrench the heteronormative and cisnormative discourse of the school. This is an example of institutional erasure, as illustrated in Figure 1 above.

The leadership team at the school profess to be actively pursuing an agenda of inclusion based on conservative Catholic pedagogy. They claim to be working to address the persistent gendering of bathroom facilities, stating that any new toilets built in the future will be designed such that they will not 'need' to be gendered, and working towards rebadging some of the current toilets to unisex. They also make assurances that the uniform options will be adapted in the near future, and that any student may currently request to wear the uniform options with which they feel most comfortable. The practice of conducting certain classes, and other activities such as camps, along binary gender lines is also receiving attention, as is the gathering of information from students and teachers regarding gender identification.

Conclusions on 'naturalness'

The school plays an important role in the life of any child. Most Australian children will undergo thirteen years (including preschool) of compulsory education, through which they will be moulded as citizens. The unexamined school environment constructs, regulates and reinforces binary divisions both through the physical construction of the environment, and through the discourses governing classroom participation and curricular content. In this sense, the network of power 'involves multiple processes, patterns, origins and location which overlap, repeat or imitate one another, support one another, distinguish themselves from one another according to their domain of application' (Foucault 1977, p. 173). Challenging assumptions about the 'naturalness' of binary gender identity is integral to providing safe and inclusive learning environments, where multiplicities of gender and sexual identities are affirmed, and no longer marginalised. Schools have the capacity to disrupt the normative hegemonic discourse through attention to: the physical environment; classroom discourse; gender neutral uniform options; diversity of curricular content and adequate data collection, thus acknowledging, exploring and celebrating the diverse experiences of those previously marginalized.

References

ACARA 2009, *National Report on Schooling in Australia*, viewed 2 September 2018, <https://www.acara.edu.au/reporting/nrosia2009/national-policy-context/educational-goals>.

Bauer, G et al. 2009, "I don't think this is theoretical; this is our lives': How erasure impacts health care for transgender people', *Journal of the Association of Nurses in AIDS Care*, vol. 20, no. 5, pp. 348-361.

Blackless, M et al. 2000, 'How sexually dimorphic are we? Review and synthesis', *American Journal of Human Biology*, vol. 12, no. 2, pp. 151-166.

Butler, J 1990, *Gender trouble*, RoutledgeFalmer, New York.

Clark, T. C et al, 2013, *Youth'12 Overview: The health and wellbeing of New Zealand secondary school students in 2012*, The University of Auckland, Auckland, New Zealand.

Connell, R.W. 1995, *Masculinities*, Allen and Unwin, Sydney.

Cumming-Potvin, W & Martino, W 2018, 'Countering heteronormativity and cisnormativity in Australian schools: Examining English teachers' reflections on gender and sexual diversity in the classroom', *Teaching and Teacher Education*, vol. 74, pp. 35-48.

Durie, J 2003, 'Speaking the silence of whiteness', *Journal of Australian Studies*, vol. 27, iss. 79, pp. 135-142.

Edmund Rice Education Australia 2017, *EREA Safe and Inclusive Learning Communities Statement*, viewed 4 September 2018, <https://www.erea.edu.au/docs/default-source/about-erea/safe-and-inclusive-learning-communities/erea_safe_and_inclusive_statement.pdf?sfvrsn=2>.

Foucault, M 1977, *Discipline and punish: the birth of the prison* 1st American edition, Pantheon Books, New York.

Henry, S 2017, 'Education, queer theology and spiritual development: disrupting heteronormativity for inclusion in Jewish, Muslim and Christian faith schools', *International Journal of Children's Spirituality*, vol. 23, iss. 1, pp. 3-16.

Jones, T & Hillier, L 2013, 'Comparing trans-spectrum and same-sex attracted youth in Australia: increased risks, increased activisms', *Journal of LGBT Youth*, vol. 10, iss. 4, pp. 287-307.

McRuer, R 2006, *Crip theory: cultural signs of queerness and disability*, New York University Press, New York.

Meyer, E 2010, *Gender and sexual diversity in schools*, Springer Science and Business Media.

Mitchell, A et. al., 2014, *5th national survey of Australian secondary students and sexual health 2013*, Australian Research Centre in Sex Health and Society, La Trobe University, Melbourne.

Moreton-Robinson, A 2006, 'Towards a new research agenda?', *Journal of Sociology*, vol. 42, iss. 4, pp. 383-395.

NSW Department of Education n.d., *School Uniform Policy*, viewed 4 September 2018, <https://education.nsw.gov.au/policy-library/policies/school-uniform-policy>.

NSW Department of Education Legal Issues Bulletin 55, *Transgender Students in Schools—Legal rights and responsibilities*, viewed 2 September 2018, < https://education.nsw.gov.au/about-us/rights-and-accountability/media/documents/public-legal-issues-bulletins/LIB-55-Transgender-students-in-schools-legal-rights-and-responsibilities.pdf>

Pontecorva, C. 1997, 'Classroom Discourse for the Making of Learning' in Davies, B & Corson, D (eds) *Oral Discourse and Education. Encyclopedia of Language and Education*, vol. 3, Springer, Dordrecht.

Sex Discrimination Amendment: Sexual Orientation, Gender Identity and Intersex Status Act, 2013.

Sullivan, N 2003, *A critical introduction to queer theory*, New York University Press, New York.

Warner, M 1993, *Fear of a queer planet: queer politics and social theory*, University of Minnesota Press, Minneapolis.

Craig Middleton &
Nikki Sullivan

KINQ—Knowledge Industries Need Queering

The KINQ Manifesto

Heteronormativity has too long had the world in its grips and our mission is to prise open its fingers. Heteronormativity, we suggest, is a hereditary disposition. A set of well-trodden paths leading to tacitly agreed objects and outcomes. The more we uncritically follow these paths that are given to us, the more normalised they become, the more 'right' they seem, and the more other possible paths become unimaginable.

KINQ needs YOU to make visible and denaturalise the insidious routes that heteronormativity has us take, and to open up spaces for experimentation, for queer curation! The KINQ Manifesto is the ongoing product of all its agents. As such, it is necessarily incomplete, heterogeneous, polyvocal: it works against conventional notions of authority and ownership, of 'the manifesto'. The KINQ Manifesto may well be what Derrida (2006) describes as a 'messianicity without messianism': a call, a promise of an independent future for what is (and will always be) *to come*.

1. We, the agents of KINQ have solemnly resolved, in the name of queer praxis, to broaden the definition of sex

Sex, says Jennifer Tyburczy (2016), is more than a relationship between bodies. Sex is 'a diverse, dynamic, interactive, and interdependent social relation cultivated by the ways in which bodies, spaces, and objects interrelate' (2016, p.1). In other words, far from being natural, sex should be thought of as choreographed by convention: bodies/body-subjects are oriented (invited, coerced, positioned, and take up positions) around, towards and away from particular objects' (2016, p.1). These 'objects' can be physical (bathrooms, cars, high heels, body hair, footballs), but also, as Sara Ahmed reminds us 'objects of thought, feeling, and judgement, as well as objects in the sense of aims, aspirations, and objectives' (2006, p.56).

2. All museums are sex museums!

As Jennifer Tyburczy's landmark text *Sex Museums* clearly illustrates, all museums shape relations between bodies, spaces, and objects. They do so by reproducing, and sometimes subverting, conventional ways of seeing, knowing, and being.

Think about the ways in which museums literally orient visitors through spaces. Not only do they map out the path, they construct particular ways of moving as im/proper. Floors are not painted with running tracks, there are no hurdles, no high jumps, no interactive dance floors, no glory holes—at least, not in the museums that we've visited! Visitors are not encouraged to run, jump, or dance, in fact they are actively discouraged from it. As Dewdney, Dibosa and Walsh write of Tate Britain, 'social reserve, silence, and restrained body movement is still the tacit mode of observance' (2013, p.10). The exceptions are spaces—usually for children—that are consciously designed to encourage these kinds of activities, but only within clearly designated zones.

Think about the kinds of relationships museums establish between visitors and the objects on display. Most employ a 'look, but don't touch' ethos, (a message conveyed in signage and also through the use of cordons and glass cases) which constructs one way of interacting with, or relating to objects as correct, and others as 'off limits'.

Think about the ways in which stories are told both physically through the placement of objects in relation to others, textually in labels and wall text, and verbally through audio guides, tours, and so on. These configure particular kinds of relationships between space, bodies and objects as natural or 'normal' (family structures, typologies of being, social hierarchies) such that they appear natural, become taken-for-granted, and thus not subject to critical engagement.

3. Museums are complicit in the heteronormative disciplining of sex, in constructing frameworks of sexual normalcy

While to some GLAM sector practitioners this claim may seem surprising, to most queer-identified people it probably requires little or no explaining. But we want this claim to be a reminder that if sex refers to the relationship between bodies, objects and spaces, then 'sexual normalcy' is always also a matter of gender, class, race, dis/ability, and so on. It is always already about hierarchical relations of power. It is always about what has become invisible or seemingly 'natural' and uncontestable. If, given this, we think of queer curatorship as imperative, this imperative must necessarily be grounded, as Kama La Mackerel, Syrus Marcus Ware, Lacie Burning and others have argued, in intersectionality (cited in Barbu, 2018).

4. Museums have operated as institutions that have helped define sexual deviancy

Depictions, representations, and interpretations of heterosexuality and cisgender are ubiquitous in museums. As such their status as natural, as normal, is reaffirmed. 'Queer' identities, relations, knowledges, however, are largely absent from museum interpretation: they are rarely displayed as paths to follow. Queer ways of being are thus constituted as deviations from the norm. While such exclusions may not explicitly prohibit queer sex they function as what Sara Ahmed, in her wonderful work of KINQ scholarship *Queer Phenomenology* refers to as 'straightening devices' that keep things in line, in part by 'holding things in place' (2006, p.66). These devices (which include absence) frame queer sex as a failure to follow the straight and narrow, as off-line, deviant, perverted and perverting. As Barbara Kirshenblatt-Gimblett reminds us, 'display not only shows and speaks, it does' (cited in Tyburczy, 2016, p.2), and what heteronormative display does is to define and reaffirm sexual normalcy through the exclusion of that which it constitutes as 'other'.

5. KINQ renounces the straight and narrow

LGBTQ lives are no longer wholly absent in museums, in fact, they are increasingly included. However, inclusion in the museum often means inclusion within the parameters of sexual normalcy. One-off exhibitions for example are often characterised by a focus on histories, rights, and political struggles that employ a progressivist narrative culminating in 'victories' such as same-sex marriage. This highlighting of lives that have been excluded from mainstream narratives and institutions undoubtedly has value but at the same time it can tend to reproduce deeply held assumptions that are, for many queer-identified people, problematic. These include the normalising idea that 'homosexuality' is an ahistorical, universal, thing-in-itself, rather than an umbrella term for a range of diverse identities and practices that has been constructed, contested, lived and experienced in multiple and complex ways. This assumption, and the associated idea that liberation, equality, visibility, and inclusion in the mainstream are the ultimate goals, constitute what Lisa Duggan (2004) calls homonormativity. Homonormativity Duggan writes, is:

A politics that does not contest dominant heteronormative assumptions and institutions, but upholds and sustains them, while promising the possibility of a demobilized gay constituency and a privatized, depoliticized gay culture anchored in domesticity and consumption (Duggan, 2004, p.50).

Homonormativity, one might argue, then, follows the path of heteronormativity, and in doing so, reinforces its status as the right and proper way. At the same time, it constructs those who won't or can't follow the straight and narrow, as perverted. So whilst married, monogamous, white, middle-class, able-bodied 'respectable', gay and lesbian couples may be appearing more and more in museums; polyamory, kink, gender queerness, communal living, intergenerational relations and so on remain conspicuous in their absence.

6. KINQ sings the praises and critiques the limits of 'queer curatorship'

Jennifer Tyburczy articulates queer curatorship as a mode of display that puts non-normative principles into practice. Queer curatorship is, as she describes it, at once a critical engagement with the ways in which museums place objects in normative sexual relationships through repetition of familiar arrangements, juxtapositions, and chronologies, and a method for experimenting with object arrangements toward the development of alternative relationships. Queer curatorship, as Videofag's Jordan Tannahill and Willian Ellis demonstrate, may well have less to do with LGBTQ visibility than with 'examining gentrification, colonization, patriarchy, immigration policy… sex work, systematic racism and so on' (cited in Barbu, 2018). In short, then, there is no blue-print for queer curatorship. Nor can there be, not least because museums are diverse and situated as are their audiences, and ways of knowing, being and doing are complex, heterogeneous and multifaceted. Queer curatorship—we hope—is not the basis on which to found hierarchies of queerness, but rather, a heterogeneous, open-ended process of creative critical praxis to which we can all contribute and from which we can all learn.

Background: How did the KINQ Manifesto come about?

Concerns for equality and diversity have been increasingly shifting from the edges to the centre of museum thinking and practice over the past two decades (Sandell & Nightingale, 2013, p.1). This includes widespread recognition of the fact that the stories and experiences of lesbian, gay, bisexual, transgender, intersex, and queer (LGBTIQ+) people are largely absent in museums internationally and need to be included. While we believe that the work that has been done in this intellectual vein is undoubtedly important it often fails to critically engaging with normative ways of being, seeing, and doing in museums, and as such reaffirming the structural inequalities that underpin them including their role in assimilating difference.

Consequently, we are more interested in 'queering the museum' than in arguing for inclusion although, in saying this, we do not want to apply that the two are necessarily mutually exclusive. Or that activists, artists and practitioners need to choose between the two. On June 4th 2018 our alter egos *Foxxy '99' Peel* (Craig) and *Maxwell 'the Saint' Steed-Powers* (Nikki) enacted the first performance of the KINQ Manifesto at the Museums Galleries Australia National Conference in Melbourne, the theme of which was 'Agents of Change'. Foxy & Maxwell are agent provocateurs, part of a militantly queer international network that works tirelessly, day and night, to infiltrate the faceless behemoth that is heteronormativity. KINQ is the network's name: cultural espionage is its game.

But why a manifesto? The Encyclopedia Britannica online defines a manifesto as a document publicly declaring the position of its issuer, criticising a present state of affairs, and advancing an alternative view and/or plan of action. Inspired by the political commitment and vehemence found in manifestos, this is what the KINQ Manifesto set out to achieve, at least in its initial iteration. However, our discomfort with manifestos is that they tend to be didactic, univocal, closed, and unchanging (in much the same way that museum interpretation has been). While we have undoubtedly been inspired by the political. The KINQ Manifesto is open to *critique*, to *change*, to *iteration*. It will, we hope, work towards and embody 'queerness', whatever that might mean.

What next?

The next phase of KINQ will open up the manifesto, the ideas it presents, to a broad audience to critique, comment, and share. This will take the form on an online forum, a blog. If you are interested in contributing head to kinqblog.wordpress.com and contact us.

KINQ wants you!

References

Ahmed, Sara (2006), *Queer Phenomenology: Orientations, Objects, Others*, Durham: Duke University Press.

Barbu, Adam (2018) 'Queer Curating, from Definition to Deconstruction', *Canadian Art*, April 4, https://canadianart.ca/features/queer-curating/ Accessed 15 July 2018.

Derrida, Jacques (2006) *Spectres of Marx: The State of Debt, the Work of Mourning and the New International*, London: Routledge.

Dewdney, Andrew, David Dibosa & Victoria Walsh (2013) *Post-critical Museology: Theory and Practice in the Art Museum*, London: Routledge.

Duggan, Lisa (2004), 'The New Homonormativity: The Sexual Politics of Neoliberalism', in Csatronovo & Nelson (eds.), *Materializing Democracy: Toward a Revitalized Cultural Politics*, Durham: Duke University Press, pp.175-94.

Marinetti, Filippo Tommaso (1909). *The Futurist Manifesto*, https://www.societyforasianart.org/sites/default/files/manifesto_futurista.pdf accessed 16 Octover 2018

Munro, Andre (2012), 'Manifesto' in *Encyclopedia Britannica online*, https://www.britannica.com/topic/manifesto accessed 16 October 2018.

Nightingale, Eithne and Sandell, Richard (eds.) (2012), 'Introduction', in Sandell and Nightingale (eds.), *Museums, Equality and Social Justice*, London: Routledge, pp.1-9.

Solanas, Valerie (1967). *The SCUM Manifesto*, http://kunsthallezurich.ch/sites/default/files/scum_manifesto.pdf accessed 16 October 2018.

Tyburczy, Jennifer (2016), *Sex Museums: The Politics and Performance of Display*, Chicago: University of Chicago Press.

Watkin, Christopher (n.d.) 'Explaining Derrida with Diagrams 2: Messianicity without messianism', https://christopherwatkin.com/2017/03/08/explaining-derrida-diagrams-2-messianicity-without-messianism/ Accessed 05 October 2018.

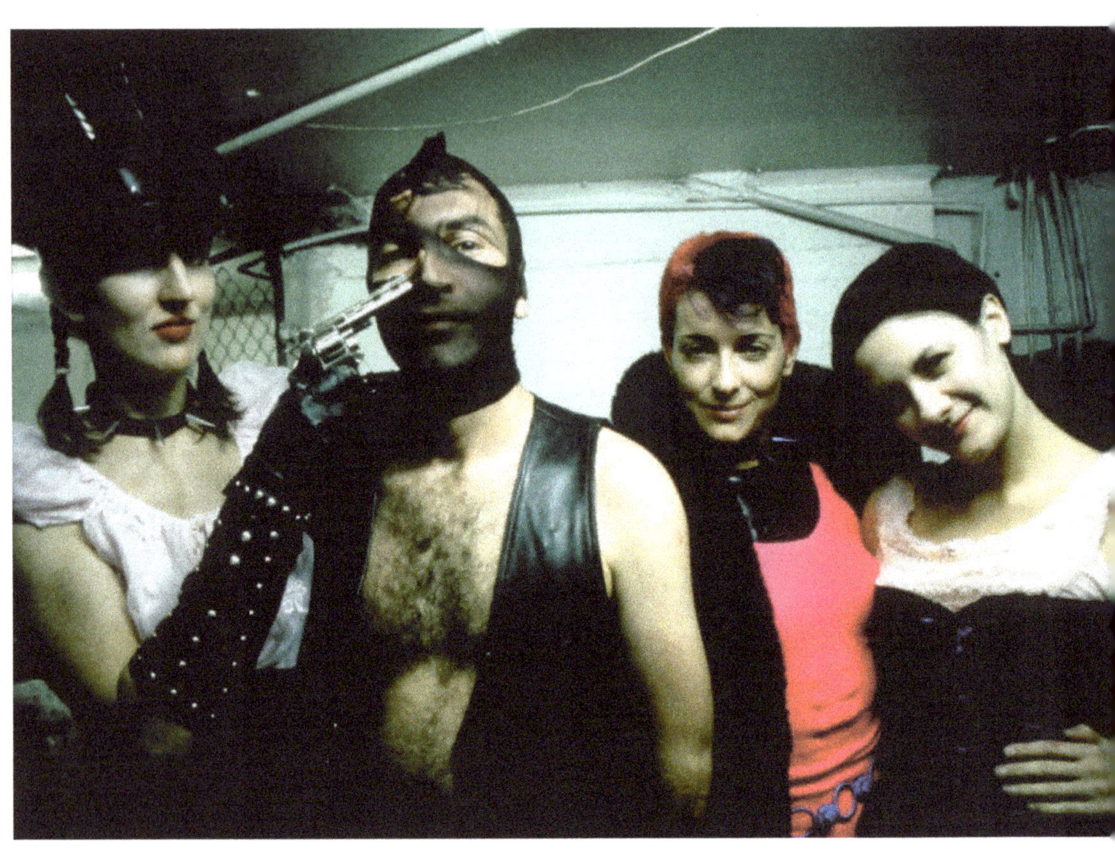

JAMIE JAMES | Dressing room, Hellfire, Blackmarket, Chippendale
1994

going Hellfire

midweek 1991 a friend's house LA Law on the TV
Episode 512 C.J. and Abby kiss we cheer and bliss
even though that's all we get (ratings beat story
every time ratings make sure dyke love stays chaste)

dyke love is faux fur coat black corset
lipstick smash eyeliner slash
a rouched cotton top a keening gun
boots that know how to dance and kick how to run

he adored us fell for us went Hellfire for us caressed
a shining barrel dropped down again again for us
dropped under stomped boots torn stocking on head
not an utter of anything but yes

fast daylight slide film lets us uncrisp, lets us inside
the blur, makes a line more than itself

then chemical baths warm solutions
acetic acid for permanence for light resistance
skin turned darkroom slippy a low burn
like that quickened LA Law kiss

dyke love is more than this

QUINN EADES

Maria Pallotta-Chiarolli
Safe spaces, inclusive services

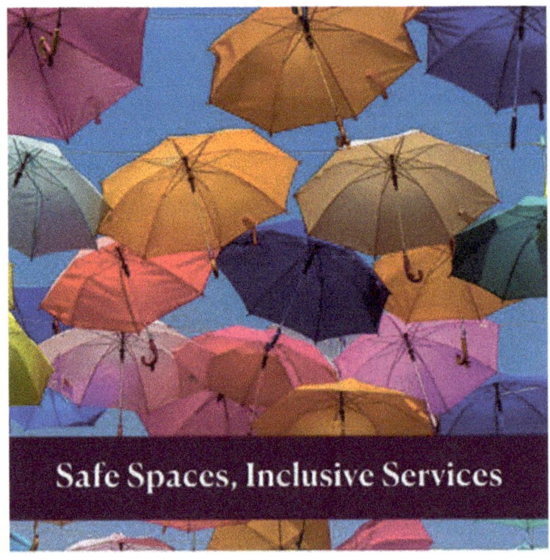

Safe Spaces, Inclusive Services—support service access and engagement by LGBTIQ+ Muslims, *by Dr Maria Pallotta-Chiarolli, was published June 2018 by Muslim Collective, Melbourne. Following is an excerpt from the executive summary.*

In 2017, Muslim Collective received funding from the Multicultural Affairs and Social Cohesion Division (MASC) in the Victorian State Department of Premier and Cabinet (DPC) to conduct a research project aimed at improving our understanding of the unique service needs and delivery requirements for vulnerable members of the Muslim LGBTIQ+ community.

The rationale behind this research is the knowledge that many Muslim LGBTIQ+ people want to belong to and feel they have a place in their families and faith. Community, faith and health services can play an important role in supporting LGBTIQ+ Muslims in navigating this space.

While the dominant heteronormative discourse of Islam constructs same-sex attraction and gender diversity as problematic (and perhaps imposed by a 'morally decadent' West) there are marginalised alternative interpretations that provide more nuanced perspectives. Some LGBTIQ+ Muslims also differentiate between religion and spirituality. In this way, many LGBTIQ+ Muslims continue to meaningfully identify as Muslims (both in religion and ethno-cultural identity).

LGBTIQ+ Muslims experience complex discrimination and prejudice in the form of micro-aggressions that remind them of the constant threats they face. This has been exacerbated by globalisation and social media whereby the assaults can be experienced vicariously.

In this report, we explore participants' experiences of how their sexualities, gender identities and religious beliefs affect their healthcare access and use, and the meanings they derive from such experiences. While exploring how LGBTIQ+ Muslims address and manage stresses can provide practical insight into means of promoting resilience and encouraging the access of health and community services, it does not excuse or decrease structural and institutional responsibility and culpability.

The study involved qualitative interviews with members of the LGBTIQ+ Muslim community. It was conducted in accordance with decolonising research design and practice and the Guidelines for Muslim Community-University Research Partnerships published by the Islamic Council of Victoria (ICV) (2017). This Report is therefore an example of and recommends co-design, coparticipation, co-review and coimplementation research strategies which enhance trust in and the credibility of the researchers. In adopting all the above ethics and methods for this research, the aim was to prevent participants feeling exploited and to avoid their homogenisation into a single queer Muslim representation. Hence, this report is provided with mindfulness regarding the considerable diversity of religious teachings and practices, cultures and languages within the categorization of 'Muslim community'.

Research findings

LGBTIQ+ Muslims often experience discrimination against their sexuality by their faith community, and against their faith, by the LGBTIQ+ and broader communities. This 'border positionality' of LGTBIQ+ Muslims makes it more difficult to access a wide range of services including general medical services, specialist medical services (including mental health services), community support services (including pastoral care) and crisis services (homelessness). Our findings indicate that approaches to service engagement vary depending on personal experiences and knowledge of services available.

One overarching finding was the need to engage and educate all members of society: non-Muslim health practitioners need to better engage and understand the Muslim faith, and Muslim community members and practitioners need to broaden their understanding of social justice and equality to include LGBTIQ+ Muslims. While services that offer LGBTIQ+ support are dedicated to providing their services in a non-discriminatory fashion, there is a perception (some of it experientially driven) that non-white queer identities are still not supported and LGBTIQ+ services remain stringently non-spiritual spaces. Participants call for health services to be conducive to addressing and affirming the significance of spiritual health where they can meet and have discussions with Islamic scholars and explore ways to reconcile their faith with their sexuality.

Many LGBTIQ+ Muslims reluctantly adopt strategies of compartmentalisation, whereby specific identities are either made publicly visible or given importance, or concealed or undermined depending on the context, necessity or safety. The decompartmentalisation of these identities is the predominant proposition of how services can be improved. Some participants believe specifically addressing LGBTIQ+ issues by religious leaders is not required as long as they address all specific examples of marginalisation under the same banner of social justice, peace and duty of care.

Encouraging the wider Muslim community to affirm LGBTIQ+ members will help prevent the 'shame' and 'ostracism' that individual families of LGBTIQ+ members experience. It is believed that families also need support groups and services in how to foster the health and wellbeing of their LGBTIQ+ members.

Participants believe that support service providers do not have to be Muslim but they need to have a respect and understanding of the faith and not perceive it as a coerced identity, or irreconcilable with an LGBTIQ+ identity. Not all LGBTIQ+ Muslims are ready to come out or let people in, and disclosing one's sexuality to a Muslim healthcare provider is often considered a threatening exposure to the Muslim community. Similarly, participants describe judgement from the LGBTIQ+ community for staying 'in the closet'.

Participants call for issue-specific health services to be more aware of and cater for LGBTIQ+ ethno-religious interfaces. Sexual health services are identified as a specific sector requiring attention. Young Muslims are often ridiculed (sometimes even by health workers) for their lack of sexual knowledge and this discourages them from seeking further support. Participants suggest making sexual health education available in schools (including Islamic schools) in a culturally competent way. There are similar expressions with regards to mental health services, which also tend to "white-wash" clients in dominant cultural expectations.

The media has played an increasingly salient role in framing Muslims negatively (terrorism, illegal migration, homophobia) which increases the alienation from wider Australian policies, culture and services for LGBTIQ+ communities. LGBTIQ+

Muslims experience increasing fear of voicing their needs and realities in mainstream media for fear of retaliation and international exposure to diasporic families with unintended harmful consequences. Media industries need to be mindful of these fears when engaging LGBTIQ+ Muslims for personal narratives.

Positive experiences in non-Muslim LGBTIQ+ services include feeling welcome, understood and empowered. Negative experiences occur if the service does not affirm or engage with the realities and concerns of the client, and makes assumptions rather than asks questions about specific life circumstances.

Muslim LGBTIQ+ organisations are often limited in capacity due to a lack of resourcing and funding but provide a significant service in fostering a sense of community and support, as well as providing the space for spiritual dialogue.

Non-LGBTIQ+ Muslim organizations (such as Muslim Collective and ICV) provide spaces for engagement with diverse faith perspectives.

Participants identify the need for accommodation and other crisis services for LGBTIQ+ refugees and asylum seekers and for Muslims who come out to their families (or friends if they are house-sharing), and have been forced to leave. Wider community settlement and crisis services address very fundamental needs for living, such as food, housing, medical care, education and employment, framed by social, mental and emotional support, but the services need to better cater for LGBTIQ+ Muslim needs.

Participants report that there was not enough awareness of services available and this should be addressed through targeted strategies (within organisations and online).

Participants believe that it is important to delineate between the different types of Muslim religious and community leadership: official and unofficial, theological and social, family-centred and organization-centred.

Participants want a discreet and financially and geographically accessible physical location (that is not a 'typical gay' venue) where they can come together and discuss their LGBTIQ+ realities interwoven with various other community issues. A major reason given is the construct of a communal space being a Muslim cultural tradition.

The lack of LGBTIQ+ Muslim health workers and their employment by wider health services is identified as a strong barrier. Participants are also concerned that LGBTIQ+ services justify their lack of Muslim workers with the reluctance of the latter to want to work in their organisations.

The full report Safe Spaces, Inclusive Services—support service access and engagement by LGBTIQ+ Muslims *can be found (with space for comment and feedback) at https://www.muslimcollective.com/embrace-research*

Dennis Altman

A locked closet: LGBTI rights around the world

In over 70 countries homosexual behaviour remains illegal; in some of these—and indeed in some countries with apparently progressive legislation—rape, murder and torture are the potential fate of people who appear to flout conventional gender and sex roles.

Over the past decade there has been increased scapegoating by authoritarian states of lesbian, gay, bisexual, transgender and intersex (LGBTI) behaviour, often linked to the growth of fundamentalist religiosity. Every now and then such moves attract international attention, as in moves to introduce the death penalty for homosexuality in Uganda; increasing violence against queers in Russia; the apparent murder of homosexuals in Syria and Iran; and draconian persecutions in Chechnya.

Of course, there have been some gains for queer movements, and encouraging signs of activism in very difficult environments, such as Tunisia and Kenya. It seems likely that the Indian Supreme Court will finally strike down Section 377, which would have repercussions across the Commonwealth. The United Nations Human Rights Council has appointed an Independent Expert to report on protection against violence and discrimination based on sexual orientation and gender expression. But I can't endorse Peter Tatchell's claim that: 'Overall, LGBTI rights are mostly powering ahead.'

Perhaps most disheartening are increasing attacks on 'LGBT people' in two countries, Turkey and Indonesia, long seen as centres of moderate and tolerant Islam. Over the past few years

Indonesian homosexuals have been targeted, with police, vigilantes and government officials attacking them as hostile to national values. Currently there are moves in the Indonesian parliament to criminalise consensual sex outside marriage, which includes any homosexual sex. The backlash against 'gay rights' is matched in many other countries, where discussion of sexual rights has become conflated with neo-liberal imperialism.

The rise of populist authoritarianism and the decline of a commitment to human rights as part of universal political discourse threatens to undermine the gains we think we've made. In countries such as South Africa and Brazil, which had seemed to lead in their acceptance of diverse sexualities, the growth of fundamentalist religious and nationalist movements is a major factor. The 'illiberal democracy' of Viktor Orbán is matched by the decline of democracy in countries such as Poland, the Philippines and Thailand. Even where authoritarian regimes do not invoke homosexuality and/or gender ideology as a threat—it does not seem to be part of the current nationalistic authoritarianism of China—they are very unlikely to be sympathetic to rights claims.

When Jon Symons and I explored some the apparent polarisation around queer rights in our book *Queer Wars* we anticipated, perhaps too easily, that Clinton would be the next United States (US) President, and that American support for global LGBTI initiatives would continue. Former Secretary of State Tillerson stressed there is a difference between policies and values, and his incoming successor will be even less sympathetic to claims for human rights. US funding for LGBTI organisation is declining, as is active US support for international organisations generally. Maybe there is an advantage in queer rights not being a football in a new Cold War but having Putin and Trump on the same side is worse than having them opposed.

Western queer movements have been largely uninterested in global developments, although there are a number of organisations working to support queer movements in countries with political and religious barriers to greater acceptance. Small groups of queer activists have brought these issues into events like Sydney Mardi Gras, but our attention has tended to be fragmentary and transitory. Where Australian queer groups have developed genuine links with overseas groups, as is true in the HIV sector, these tend to be managed very tightly by small groups of insiders. Sometimes responses seem more motivated by a desire to feel good than any thought through strategy to assist people in desperate situations; one of the organisers of a demonstration last year against horrific abuses of basic rights in Chechnya told me that it made the participants feel good. It is not easy to work out the best way to support people in countries where obvious western support may well boomerang and reinforce attacks on queers as the imposition of western values.

This is not to discount the importance of using international institutions to consistently support measures to protect people from violence and persecution based on sexuality and gender expression. It is heartening that in his statement to the Human Rights Council (HRC) marking Australia's election to the body, Governor General Peter Cosgrove committed to 'strong advocacy for equal human rights, non-discrimination and non-violence for LGBTI persons.' But as the Australian government ignores HRC views on offshore detention it can hardly complain if other states ignore our position on queer rights.

Many of the United Nations agencies have been creative in supporting initiatives around these issues, and Australian support is increasingly important as the US withdraws from the field. Such support needs to be supplemented by much stronger links between regional queer groups and their Australian counterparts. In particular, there are two areas where Australia could do more.

First, the flow of people seeking asylum because of their sexuality and gender expression will increase; we need do all we can to increase the rate at which claims for asylum are accepted. No country has a particularly good record on welcoming queer asylum seekers, and Australia has certainly granted asylum to a number of people on these grounds. Given the current asylum regime one can only hope that the Immigration Department—now part of Peter Dutton's Home affairs Empire—recognises the complexities of establishing asylum claims based on sexual and gender discrimination.

Second, two years ago the Australian Council for International Development adopted a series of measures to ensure acknowledgement of persecution based on sexuality and gender expression amongst its member organisations. Given the number of religious-based NGOs delivering forms of overseas assistance this is a major step forward, although the sector has been slow to fully implement this commitment. There is enormous need to work with the big international development non-governmental organisations—particularly those like World Vision with a religious base—to increase their ability to understand queer issues and incorporate them into their overall development work. Often these are the most significant Australian presence in developing countries.

At the recent Commonwealth Heads of Government Meeting there was some focus on the realities for queer people (a majority of Commonwealth countries, including those most adept at anti-colonial rhetoric, still maintain nineteenth century British prohibitions on homosexual behaviour). I doubt if Theresa May's words will change the minds of any leaders present, but airing the issue gives support to local activists. As one of the protagonists in the film *Mr Gay Syria* says, 'Out of despair comes hope'.

Article originally published by the Australian Institute of International Affairs (http://www.internationalaffairs.org.au/australianoutlook/a-locked-closet-lgbti-rights/) 26 Apr 2018.

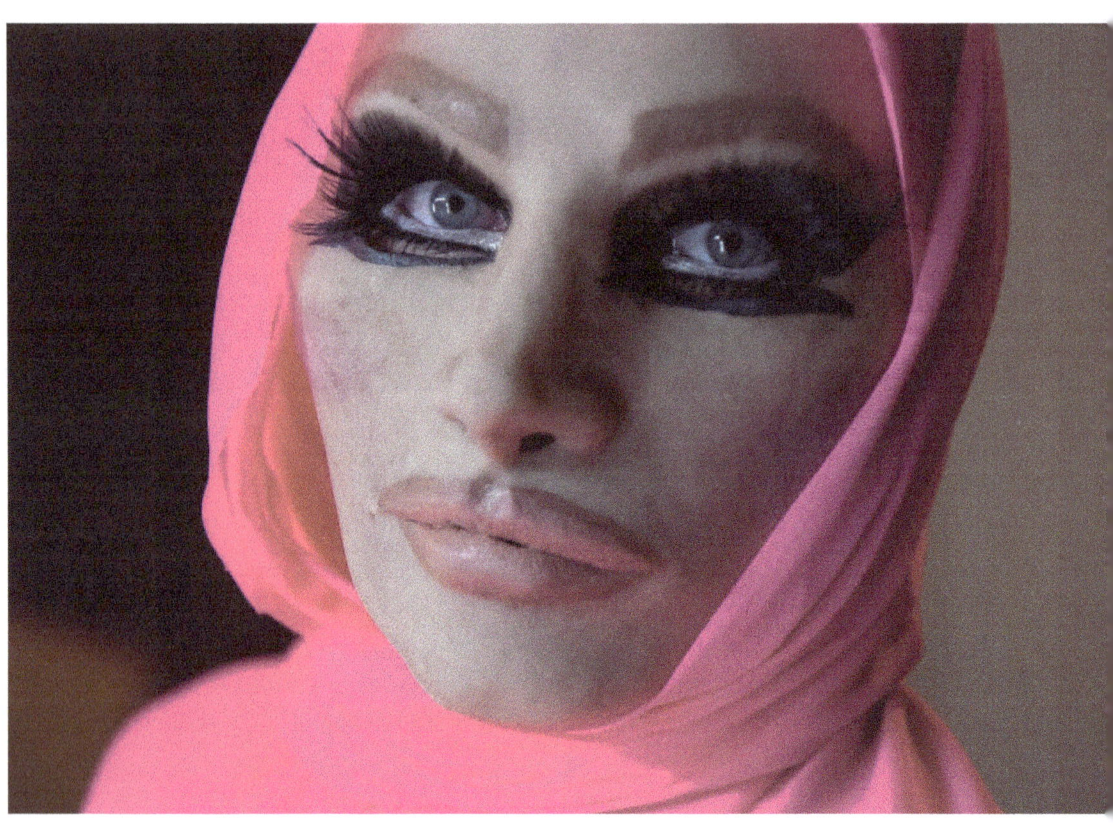

JAMIE JAMES | Dallas Dellaforce, Queer Central, Imperial Hotel, Erskineville 2018.

hustling the mirror

what is it about drag lipstick
how it pushes up and over peaks
how it aims at the septum
how it makes me want to push my tongue
in all the way to kiss

lashes are birdwings those bottom lids
a silvered landing place

a gaze that goes right through

a single source of light

you wouldn't know this was a hot and tiny
dressing room holding a cluster of queens
drawing eyebrows with fat pencils
and hustling the only mirror

land on these lids
kiss those lips
wrap yourself in a sybaritic scarf
be sung to sleep by eyelash flicker and breath

QUINN EADES

Janet Rice

A year ago today

Facebook post, 7 December 2018

A year ago today, legislation for marriage equality passed the Australian parliament.

For most of us, this was a time to celebrate that after decades of community campaigning and activism, a massive piece of state-sanctioned discrimination was finally scrubbed from our law books.

But for others, achieving marriage equality was a relief more than a celebration. It was the end of a campaign that was not necessary, that caused considerable harm and damage.

And a year on, some in our community are still recovering from the impacts of that campaign.

Today it would have been great to reflect on the achievement of marriage equality as both a momentous day in Australian history and as a turning point - the time we left homophobic and transphobic attacks resolutely behind us and looked to a brighter future for our resilient communities.

But instead there's a cloud darkening today's rainbow anniversary.

The last few months have been another challenging period for our communities. We've been subjected once again to the same awful rhetoric of the marriage campaign.

The timing with the marriage anniversary is uncanny.

I can't believe there's any 'debate' to be had over whether or not LGBTQ+ kids deserve to go to school without being bullied, expelled or discriminated against by their school.

Or that LGBTQ+ teachers and staff can be fired from the jobs they love because of who they love.

The simple fact is discrimination against LGBTQ+ people is unacceptable. It is wrong. It cannot be allowed to continue.

Schools should be discrimination-free zones for all LGBTQ+ people. Full stop. No ifs. No buts.

Time and time again, LGBTIQ+ Australians have been used as political footballs by politicians of all stripes.

We saw it when Labor did a dirty deal with John Howard to change the definition of the *Marriage Act* in 2004. We saw it during the postal survey last year. We've seen it this year from Prime Minister Scott Morrison all year, culminating this week with his reprehensible bill that would expand discrimination in schools and make conversion practices completely legal and accepted.

Well I have had enough.

I've had enough of hearing my community being talked about as if we're some kind of 'other'.

I've had enough of my community being told that our relationships and families aren't as valid as those of cisgender heterosexuals.

I've had enough of my community being told that we don't deserve to live our lives without discrimination.

Our communities are resilient and strong, but we've suffered enough.

Our communities have always had to fight for our rights and I know we'll keep working together to pressure the Morrison government and Bill Shorten's Labor party to ensure they do the right thing and make our schools discrimination-free zones.

We can make this country a better, more inclusive place right now. But that will only happen when politicians stop using us as pawns in their sick game of political point scoring and work together.

I'm proud that the Greens have always stood up for LGBTIQ+ people. I can promise you we always will.

And I'm optimistic that we will eventually remove discrimination in our schools and in society, just like we removed discrimination from marriage laws.

I'm optimistic because a poll taken when the Ruddock Review was leaked in October showed that three quarters of Australians think LGBTIQ+ people should be protected in schools.

So on this first anniversary of marriage equality passing the parliament, I hope all Australians will celebrate what was an historic day in Australian history.

But I also call on all Australians, especially cisgender, heterosexual Australians, to stand with and support LGBTIQ+ people to make sure our schools, and indeed our society, are discrimination-free zones. Full stop. No ifs. No buts.

SENATOR JANET RICE
Senator for Victoria

Geoff Allshorn

A case for rainbow atheism

We're living in the midst of a revolution in human attitudes and belief. In much of Europe and North America and other parts of the developed world, such as Australia and Japan, large portions of the population are now non-religious … This is an unprecedented moment in the history of humanity (Lindsay, 2014, p. 13).

Ours is fast becoming a godless nation. The ABS reports that since 1911, the number of Australians subscribing to 'no religion' has increased from one person out of every 250 (ABS, 2013) to what is now a little short of one in three—a breathtaking social change in just over a century. In the 2016 Census, the combined factions of our nation's dominant religion, Christianity, struggled to retain a collective majority foothold at just 52% of respondents, while other religions totalled 8%. But the largest single category of respondents was 'no religion' at 30% of the population (ABS, 2016a).[1]

How does this relate to queer people? Some 57% of same-sex couples reported having 'no religion' (ABS, 2016b),[2] suggesting that the godless population among LGBTQIA+ people may be almost double that of the Australian average—a difference which might be partly attributed to the fact that historically, religion has not been kind to queer people. We might therefore reasonably

---

[1]Note that the 'religion' question was optional in the 2016 Census; consequently, the percentage results do not total 100%.
[2]Note that the same-sex couples results are somewhat problematic, but they remain the optimal way to assess the religious views of likely LGBTQIA+ Australians.

extrapolate from census data that between approximately one-third (30%) to one-half (57%) of LGBTQIA+ communities comprise atheists and others who reject traditional religions. The possible links between godlessness and LGBTQIA+ people run deeper than even census results might suggest. Our communal histories and lived experiences reveal powerful parallels.

The historic record

History is unambiguous: our very existence as queer people signals a rejection of traditional religious and social dogmas. In his definitive book, *Homosexual: Oppression and Liberation*, Dennis Altman foreshadowed this attitudinal change:

Liberation entails not just freedom from sexual restraint, but also freedom for the fulfillment of human potential, a large part of which has been unnecessarily restricted by tradition, prejudice, and the requirements of social organisation. (Altman, 2012, p.104).

The resultant social evolution—still underway—has created what Darryl Ray (2014) calls secular sexuality, a modern lifestyle which liberates people from Christianity's historic abhorrence of sex and sexuality: 'A secular sexual is not a Christian and does not need to act like one.' Such a rejection of traditional oppression—with its implicit endorsement of individuality, independence and fabulosity—could describe both atheists and queers.

LGBT atheist Camille Beredjick (2017, p.29) conflates our communities:

Politically and personally, atheists and LGBTQ people overlap. LGBTQ people are more likely to be atheists than the general population; atheists are more likely to support LGBTQ rights. In some cases, discovering that you're LGBTQ is the spark that causes you to leave the faith in which you were raised.

Although atheism encompasses everyone from nihilists to optimists, humanism is at the optimistic end of this spectrum, and it has many atheist adherents. In the 1960s, humanists in Australia spearheaded the movement for 'homosexual law reform', and then later stepped aside in order to allow the developing gay and lesbian rights movement to claim its own autonomy. Humanism is being challenged today by those who seek to trump human rights with 'religious rights'.

Freedom of belief

There are many LBGTQIA+ people who find fulfilment within queer-friendly religious communities—and we should respect their right to do so. We should also celebrate their efforts to change homophobic doctrines and practices inside their faith networks. While standing firm against religious excesses, we must be prepared to offer believers respect in ways that their churches have historically failed to extend to us. But we should also uphold the right of queer people to disbelieve.

A recent forum on 'LGBTI Inclusion in Faith Communities' acknowledged that religion has been a source of both great solace and great anguish for LGBTI Australians (Victorian Government, 2017). Such a conclusion falls far short of providing reconciliation to LGBTQIA+ people who have been burned by religion, or to disbelievers who comprise a significant percentage of the Australian population. We need secular representation that does not rely upon the privilege of religious people to debate our civil rights. Where are the queer atheist voices in LGBTQIA+ community discourse and public debates?

Coming out

The concept of 'coming out' is well-known within LGBTQIA+ communities. US gay activist Harvey Milk—who renounced his faith at a young age (Faderman, 2018)—encouraged queer people to 'come out' as an act of both personal and political empowerment. 'Coming out' has, in recent years, also been adopted by many atheists, who, like queers, have been traditionally stigmatised by faith communities. Atheists are often pigeonholed as being different, deviant and distrusted—where have we heard that before?—and in many countries, they face danger, family rejection, and persecution. 'Coming out' is a doubly relevant act for queer atheists. How can we acknowledge and support them?

Bridge building

Gay humanist Chris Stedman calls for cooperation between the faithful and the faithless:

There are many possible answers to the question of how atheists should engage with the religious … the problems of the world are too numerous to debate it for long. We must find solidarity wherever we can—and act upon it (Stedman, 2012, Ch 7).

Such solidarity is possible, as anyone can recall who lived through our traumatic epidemic years, when renegade nuns held the hands of our dying friends. More recently, religious folk marched alongside atheists at marriage equality rallies. In a similar spirit, we must recognise the need for reconciliation today between theists and rainbow atheists. Our diversity demands no less.

References

ABS (2013). 4102.0—Australian Social Trends, Nov 2013: Losing My Religion (Introduction). 20 November 2013, at http://www.abs.gov.au/ausstats/abs@nsf/Lookup/4102.0Main+Feature30Nov+2013#introduction.

ABS (2016a). 2071.0—Census of Population and Housing: Reflecting Australia—Stories from the Census, 2016: Religion in Australia. 28/06/2017, at http://www.abs.gov.au/ausstats/abs@nsf/Lookup/by%20Subject/2071.0-2016-Main%20Features-Religion%20Data%20Summary70.

ABS (2016b). 2071.0—Census of Population and Housing: Reflecting Australia—Stories from the Census, 2016: Same Sex Couples in Australia 2016: Religious Affiliation. 28/06/2017, at http://www.abs.gov.au/ausstats/abs@nsf/Lookup/2071.0main+features852016.

Altman, D. (2012). *Homosexual: Oppression and Liberation*. Saint Lucia: University of Queensland Press.

Beredjick, C. (2017). Queer Disbelief: Why LGBTQ Equality Is an Atheist Issue. *Friendly Atheist Press*, 2017 (1).

Faderman, Lillian (2018). *Harvey Milk: His Lives and Death.* London: Yale University Press.

Lindsay, R. (2013). *The Necessity of Secularism: Why God Can't Tell Us What to Do*, Durham: Pitchstone Publishing.

Ray, D. (2014). 'Secular Sexuality: A Direct Challenge to Christianity', in John W Loftus (ed), *Christianity Is Not Great: How Faith Fails.* New York: Prometheus Books, p. 371.

Stedman, C. (2012). *Faitheist: How an Atheist Found Common Ground with the Religious.* Boston: Beacon Press.

Victorian Government (2017). *Forum on LGBTI Inclusion in Faith Communities: Statement of Support.* Melbourne: Victorian Multicultural Commission.

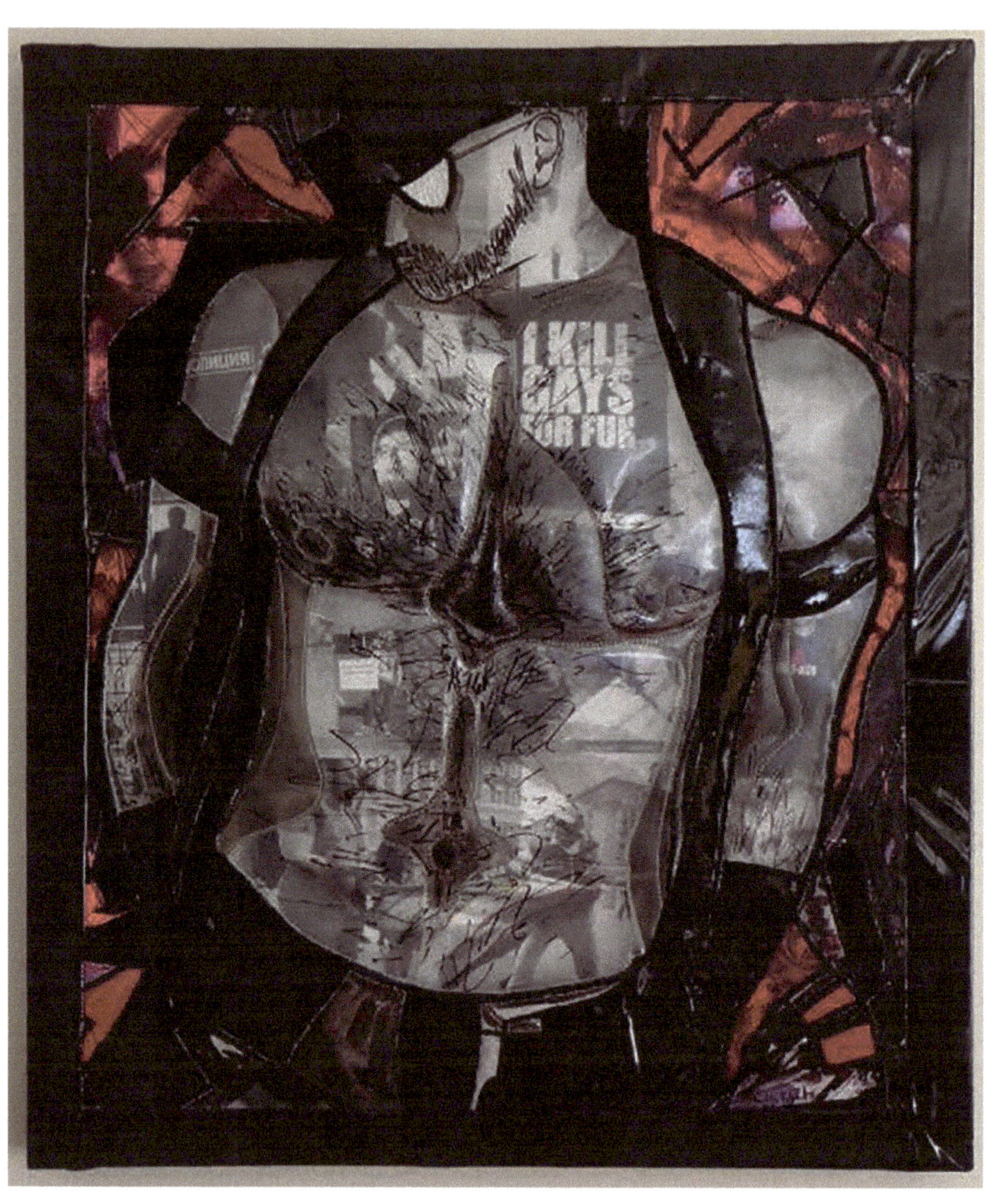

MARTIN ROBERTS | VINYL QUEEN

Martin Roberts

Ink and vinyl therapy

Martin Roberts' artwork 'Vinyl Queen' (facing page) was Highly Commended in the 2018 Bent Art Competition, and is a clever and timely piece that caught our eye. It features a luscious image at first that invites the viewer to peer in to one very attractive commercial image of a male dressed in a commodified queer aesthetic, but then the piece contrasts this initial invitation against the hate-based imagery and messaging that looks almost reflected onto his body. Martin Robert tells Bent Street *about some of the meanings and inspirations woven into his work.*

On 'Vinyl Queen'

This piece was one of a 'Drag' series of three that I did for the 2018 Bent Art exhibition. I was thinking about how the gay community is renowned for its glamorous and flamboyant posturing and drag is synonymous with the scene. Traditional understandings of a 'drag queen' are of a man who ostentatiously dresses up in women's clothes, but this could be said to extend to the many subcultures that exist within the community, from leather men and bears, to Twinks and muscle boys in footy shorts. All of this 'drag' is a form of costuming, an image presented to the world derived from fantasy as a mechanism to feel empowered and whole. Yet often in our community that's obsessed with appearance, these drag images mask our hidden traumas and insecurities.

The piece, 'Vinyl Queen' is stitched together to consider the many layers of experience that exist beyond the superficial presentations made by some of the visually striking groups that inhabit the space under the rainbow umbrella. There are two layers to the piece. The top layer is made primarily of fabric appliqué, pieces of fabric collaged together and painted on before stitching it all together. But in this piece I also used transparent coloured plastic for the areas of skin, so you can see through to an under layer of internet printouts that are collaged together and washed over with ink. Those images appear to reflect across the body, it's actually a view through to a separate under layer.

On choosing a professional art therapy career

It was really a gradual process throughout my career that led me to become a professional arts therapist. Originally I studied fashion design in the 90's, and upon graduating I went on to work mainly as a costumier for film and theatre. However in addition to working on specific productions I always liked to also use creative processes to work with people on different community projects. For instance I ran a creative fashion module in a women's prison in my home town of Dublin, Ireland that was aimed at building the confidence and self-esteem of a group of inmates there. Projects such as this sparked my interest in arts therapy and as I learnt more about the field it became apparent that it could be an area that would satisfy my desire to work with and help people, as well as using my creative skills and experience.

To become an accredited professional arts therapist you need to study a Masters of Art Therapy, which is full time over 2 years or part time over 4 years and includes a year-long clinical studies component. I studied at Western Sydney University and did the course part time as I still had to continue working. It was an amazing and inspiring course which changed my life and also had a big influence on my art.

On conducting art therapy

As an arts therapist you work collaboratively with people both individually and in groups to help them improve areas of their lives that they may be having difficulties with. Together you develop a therapeutic relationship, whereas the therapist you enable the creation of a trusting space where the client can feel safe to explore any issues they may have and address difficult emotions and traumas.

As opposed to more traditional talking therapies, with arts therapy the primary form of communication is through the arts, whether that be drawing, painting, sculpture or whatever medium the client wishes to use. The emphasis is on the process of making art and using that as a form of self-expression rather than producing a finished art piece. It can be a very powerful and less threatening way for clients to work through difficult material.

On working with LGBTIQ art therapy groups

Sexuality, coming out and developing one's identity might be key issues for some members of the LGBTIQ community. Art is a wonderful way of expressing oneself that can be a fun as well as empowering way to do this. I run one particular workshop that draws on my costume experience where I work with a group and get them to create their own expressive costume celebrating an aspect of themselves. But many in the community are also dealing with a lot of trauma and shame, resulting from the institutionalised homophobia that is prevalent in the hetero-centric society we live in, and how we've been treated both past and present. We know from neuroimaging that after an individual experiences a trauma the speech language area of the brain actual shuts down. The process of arts therapy can bypass this speech language issue and accesses the same sensory areas of the brain that encode trauma. So this type of therapy can be a particularly useful way of working with these traumatic memories.

I don't like to generalise but I do think LGBTIQ people can be more open to experimenting creatively than other groups may be. Creativity and a unique way of looking at the world is a trait associated with the community, which can help them get into the flow of a project quicker, with less anxiety around the need to conform. I think the LGBTIQ community is becoming more

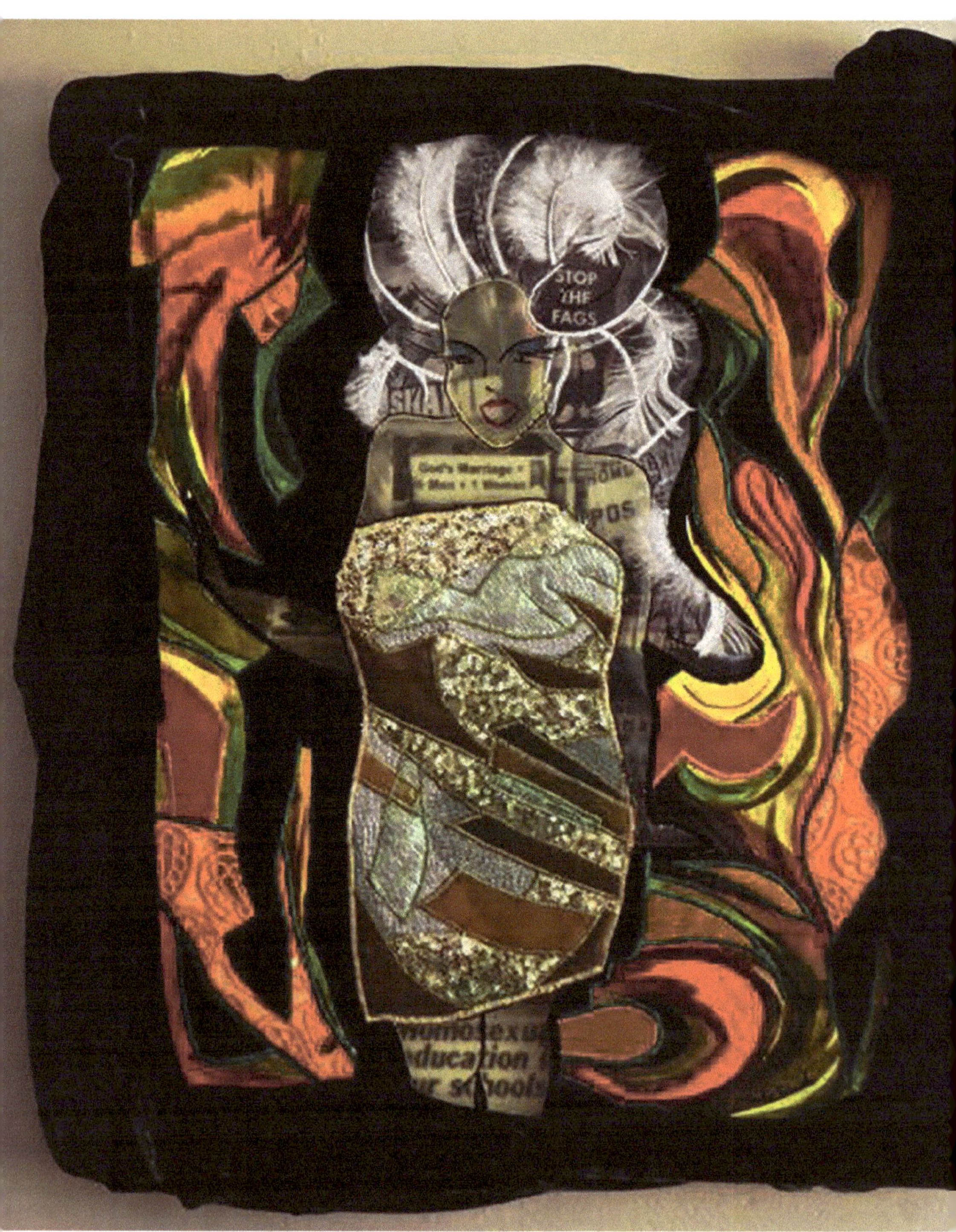
STOP
THE
FAGS

empowered and much quicker to call out the homophobia that permeates through everything. I do think there's a huge amount of trauma that hasn't been addressed and impacts the way we interact with ourselves and each other in negative ways. But things have improved immensely since I was growing up and hopefully will continue to do so.

On being an LGBTIQ artist

I've a wide taste in art and the things I'm drawn to looking at, but the two LGBTIQ visual artists that spring to mind are David Hockney and Pierres and Giles. I've an interest in the lives of different people and how they interact with each other, and also find great joy in all things kitsch. But my inspiration also comes from other sources such as popular culture and the music scene particularly from the 80s and 90s. Artists both gay and straight were more open to gender bending then in a way that isn't so much the case today and have been an ongoing inspiration to me. Issues faced by artists in the LGBTIQ community such as poor self-esteem and all the negative defence mechanisms that develop from belonging to a marginalised group affect how they interact with the world in both their professional and personal lives. So in that way they have issues that are unique to their identity. But everybody gay or straight has their own past experiences that affect them in different ways too, in fact this is often the catalyst for their creative endeavours. I'd also say that maybe those artists who choose to explore queer themes in their work might tend to be taken less seriously than other artists. But then 'Gay' art can be a particular niche that is often created for an LGBTIQ audience.

On his artistic journey and evolution

I've been making art since I was a child. After high school I went to Art College, and as I mentioned earlier ended up specialising in fashion there. I think this was partly because of my love of the different unique ways that people express themselves as well as a fascination with textiles. I've always liked making things with my hands which is probably why I was drawn to working as a costumier for many years. After each production I worked on I frequently had many beautiful scraps of left over fabrics that I couldn't bring myself to throw away. I've always liked painting and creating pictures and back in the early 2000's I started piecing those scraps of fabric together and painting on them to create artworks, over the years developing my own technique, which was essentially a form of fabric appliqué. I started to incorporate other techniques and mediums, including more painting, found objects as well as making sculptural pieces. Then studying the Masters of Art Therapy had a profound impact on my work as an artist. Although whilst studying time constraints resulted in me producing less works, with all the new concepts and theories I was learning my brain was alive and I found I was thinking about my art much more conceptually. Now my art practice is both influenced by and informs the other areas of my life, and provides me a central space of creativity and contemplation.

On LGBTIQ people starting out in art

When working with any individual or group including the LGBTIQ community, the starting point can be a bit daunting depending on their prior experiences and attitudes to art. The key is to reassure them that there's no right or wrong and help them to relax into the process. I'd usually have an array of different art materials easily available, and find that each person will be drawn to what works best for them. One individual might find coloured pencils or pens a safe and contained way to start making some marks, whereas another might be happy to dive straight into making wet messy paintings. It's really about helping each to find what they're comfortable with and how to express themselves most authentically. If people are really stuck I give them some suggestions and direction as to what they could do to get them started.

On the myth of bad art

In art therapy there is no such thing as bad art and this is something I strongly believe in. As I mentioned earlier the emphasis in arts therapy is on the process of art making rather than producing polished finished artworks. It's about exploring your experiences whilst creating and finding meaning from that. The role of the arts therapist is to create a safe environment where people can experience a state of flow in their art making and reassure them that their expressions are just as beautiful as any other persons. If you think about what is 'bad art', it's really just one person's opinion based on their own bias and social constructs. Of course we all have our own preferences of what we like in art, but in art therapy we let go of all that, and look at the actual art and what it means for the person who's made it. It's always going to be an expression from that person and that I think is a beautiful thing. In this way arts therapy can be very powerful in helping people heal from those shameful experiences when they were told they're not as good as someone else.

Roz Bellamy

Life writing as an outlet for LGBTIQA+ youth

Introduction

The first time I was taught how to write nonfiction was at a memoir workshop in Taos, New Mexico. I had only signed up because it was being taught by Emily Rapp Black. Her book about her son Ronan, and his death from Tay-Sachs disease, *The Still Point of the Turning World* (2013), is extraordinary.

On the first day of the workshop, I realised what I had signed up for. This class would not involve making things up, but instead we were meant to excavate our own experiences and bring them to life through literary and narrative techniques. I was so tentative that when I wrote my first piece, about my shuttle breaking down in the desert on the way to the workshop, I tried to come out as queer as subtly and inoffensively as possible. Of course, my classmates and Rapp Black were not about to let it go unnoticed. '*It's awesome that you were rescued by a woman*,' one of the students said. '*It's such a twist on the trope of the knight in shining armour. You were saved by a queer woman of colour. I love it*.'

Encouraged, I delved a bit deeper. I began to write about my grandfather who had died a year earlier. Writing about his life and death wasn't too raw, just bittersweet. The more I wrote, the more memories I was rewarded with, and I didn't want to leave the room.

Writing workshops take place in all sorts of spaces; some are sterile and alienating, others nurturing and cosy. The place itself and the presence of other people don't always matter. There's something else at play. When the conditions are right, the space can feel like a sanctuary.

Later, at welcome drinks, I downed several potent margaritas, forgetting that the high altitude in Taos meant I was dehydrated and that the alcohol would have a much stronger effect. I ended up inebriated but somehow felt clear-headed, and returned to my room to write. I wrote for hours, ignoring the strange sounds of a mountain town after dark and drunk writers out to play. I began to process my grief in a way that went far beyond anything experienced in therapy. This became my first published essay.

Two years later, I studied memoir writing with Cheryl Strayed, whose essay *The Love of My Life* (2002) and memoir *Wild* (2012) impacted on me in immeasurable ways. Her writing rattled me and made me see through certain layers of protection I had surrounded myself with. I had been writing fiction not because I wanted to make up characters and plots but to veil my truth, to keep myself safe. But there was Strayed, writing her truth and not veering from it, even when the truth was ugly, messy or traumatic.

Studying with these two writers led to many changes in my life, including the realisation that I could use memoir and creative nonfiction to process pain and make meaning of my experiences. Yet I wasn't completely ready to do this.

Some of my pain was associated with the bullying and exclusion I had faced during my schooling. Without properly acknowledging this, I applied for and commenced a Master of Teaching. In the subject that prepared pre-service English teachers, Associate Professor Graham Parr prompted us to write critical autobiographical narratives about our experiences with English education at school. I found the process deeply satisfying and a powerful way to release the hold the past had over me. It felt subversive to write so honestly about an institution while situated within another, but I only did it because we were instructed to do so. I was an obedient student, even when rebelling against the education system.

When I went out on placements, I wrote reflective pieces about the lessons I taught and the classes I observed. I focused on pedagogy and curriculum, taking careful notes about classroom management, which I never read again. I didn't write about the way that misbehaviour, violence, bullying, racism and sexism twisted my stomach and heightened my anxiety. I didn't write about what it felt like to be a queer and Jewish teacher and to hear anti-Semitic or homophobic comments in the majority of schools I taught in.

I began a career as a freelance writer and wrote about subjects I had previously never imagined writing about let alone publishing. I came out as bisexual and gender diverse, described a traumatic medical experience, disclosed my mental health issues, and publicly parsed interactions that I found challenging, especially when I encountered prejudice.

I started teaching high school English and Humanities. I noticed the way that the act of writing was not enjoyable for most students. The majority of the teenagers I interacted with just tolerated it. They used it because it was required for assessment purposes, but rarely as an activity that brought relaxation, peace or pleasure. I thought about implementing exciting new approaches to English teaching. I remembered the time that an experienced literature teacher, Madeleine Coulombe, presented at one of our English lectures at university to show us the literature boxes her students had been working on. The students designed and created boxes and filled them with objects, images and textual fragments associated with their writing. I also thought about the American high school teacher, Brian Mooney, who taught Kendrick Lamar's album *To Pimp a Butterfly* alongside Toni Morrison's *The Bluest Eye*.

There are so many interesting and unique ways to approach writing at school, but schools are institutions, and institutions require their subjects to adhere to rules. The nature of most school assessments, no matter how much we might want to think they are creative and playful, is mandated uniformity. Meeting the top levels of a rubric is literally about ticking off boxes, not pushing outside them or critiquing why the boxes are there in the first place.

Research

My schooling had taught me how to be an analytical writer, but not how to write reflectively, in a personal and exploratory way.

Thinking about how much I would have benefited from this sort of writing made me realise that there is an absence of life writing—including memoir, creative nonfiction, and nonfiction poetry—in educational settings. I wondered why, and what teachers and policy-makers were so worried about.

I began to read literature about narrative therapy (Pennebaker, 1997), empowerment (Laverack, 2006; Wagaman, 2016), and trauma-informed practice (Russon, 2017), and hypothesised that a therapeutic writing intervention could be adapted and related to various life writing genres. I discovered more about narrative inquiry (Richardson, 2000), various forms of life writing (Douglas & Poletti, 2016), online writing (Alexander, 2002), digital storytelling (Vivienne, 2016), self-writing/hupomnemata (Foucault, 1997), and writing as meaning-making (Hakanurmi, 2017). Through this reading, I developed an aim to design an intervention that could be used in school and wider community settings to explore identity and, in turn, promote wellbeing.

My research is interdisciplinary, bringing together perspectives and literature from education, arts, health and psychology. I am passionate about bringing a stronger focus on creativity, sense of identity, wellbeing and mental health into school settings. These are closely aligned with education policy and curriculum, which refer to all of these areas in some capacity (The Australian Ministerial Council on Education, Employment, Training and Youth Affairs [MCEETYA], 2008; Australian Curriculum, Assessment and Reporting Authority [ACARA], 2016). This requires being attentive to the ideologies, discourses and discursive gaps (Berlak & Berlak, 1981; Bernstein, 1996) embedded in curriculum and policy documents.

I thought about which population I wanted to work with, and decided that this sort of writing could be meaningful for those identifying as LGBTIQA+, despite there being a wide range of identities within this acronym. LGBTIQA+ people appear to be worse off across all indicators for mental health and wellbeing, and this is particularly the case for those experiencing harassment and violence related to their identities (Hillier et al., 2010).

The arguments used to support young LGBTIQA+ people often tend to associate queer identities with abjection or victimhood (Cover, Rasmussen, Aggleton, & Marshall, 2017), rather than focusing on empowerment, creativity, or health. Limited research has examined the way that social identities impact on meaning-making. It occurred to me that this sort of writing could be considered queer writing or queer resistance (Halberstam, 1993). I drew on queer theory (Ahmed, 2004), and considered the way that writing could mediate queer literacy (Miller, 2015) and sexual literacy (Alexander, 2008; Moje & MuQaribu, 2003).

My own sexuality and gender identity have influenced my selection of LGBTIQA+ young people as a research population; however, I would also like to look at how this research could be applied to other populations in the future. The research design has been informed by emancipatory and transformative paradigms (Mertens, 2007) and utilises decolonising research methodologies (Tuhiwai Smith, 2012) and an intersectional approach (Blackburn & Smith, 2010; Crenshaw, 1991; Lozano-Neira & Marchbank, 2016).

Conclusion

Ultimately, my research aims to examine the way that writing can reify or disrupt young LGBTIQA+ people's process of meaning-making around identity. It extends on Hakanurmi's concept of storytelling as 'a meaning-making tool for constructing identity' (2017, p. 153). Storytelling can be considered 'everyday activism' (Vivienne, 2016), which may provide an opportunity to empower marginalised young writers—including those from the LGBTIQA+ community and others—in education, publishing and wider society.

In my research, I will conduct textual analysis of the participants' writing to see how writing relates to meaning-making around identity, and perhaps whether it can ameliorate challenges such as stigma and shame. The ultimate aim is to determine whether a directed life writing intervention can be a useful process for helping people work through their identities.

In my case, the techniques and pleasures associated with life writing were introduced into my life at the age of 30. I still think about how different my schooling, and my teaching, could have been if I had learned these techniques earlier. Life writing can provide support, can be used for emotional regulation, can be cathartic, and can encourage playful exploration, all of which are often missing in mainstream approaches to secondary education.

References

Ahmed, S. (2004). *The cultural politics of emotion.* New York, NY: Routledge.

Alexander, J. (2002). Queer webs: Representations of LGBT people and communities on the world wide web. *International Journal of Sexuality and Gender Studies, 7*(2), 77-84. doi:10.1023/A:1015821431188

Alexander, J. (2008). *Literacy, sexuality, pedagogy: Theory and practice for composition studies.* Logan, UT: Utah State University Press.

Australian Curriculum, Assessment and Reporting Authority. (2016). Development of the Australian curriculum. Retrieved from https://www.acara.edu.au/curriculum/development-of-australian-curriculum

Berlak, A., & Berlak, H. (1981). *Dilemmas of schooling: Teaching and social change.* London, England: Methuen.

Bernstein, B. (1996). *Pedagogy, symbolic control, and identity: Theory, research, critique.* Washington, D.C: Taylor & Francis.

Blackburn, M. V., & Smith, J. M. (2010). Moving beyond the inclusion of LGBT-themed literature in English language arts classrooms: Interrogating heteronormativity and exploring intersectionality. *Journal of Adolescent & Adult Literacy, 53*(8), 625-634. doi:10.1598/JAAL.53.8.1

Cover, R., Rasmussen, M. L., Aggleton, P., & Marshall, D. (2017). Progress in question: The temporalities of politics, support and belonging in gender- and sexually-diverse pedagogies. *Continuum, 31*(6), 767-779. doi:10.1080/10304312.2017.1281883

Crenshaw, K. (1991). Mapping the margins: Intersectionality, identity politics, and violence against women of color. *Stanford Law Review, 43*(6), 1241–1299.

Douglas, K., & Poletti, A. (2016). *Life narratives and youth culture: Representation, agency and participation.* London, England: Palgrave Macmillan.

Foucault, M. (1997). Self writing (R. Hurley, Trans.). In P. Rabinow (Ed.), *Ethics: Subjectivity and truth* (pp. 207-222). New York, NY: The New Press.

Hakanurmi, S. (2017). Learning to work through narratives: Identity and meaning-making during digital storytelling. In G. Jamissen, P. Hardy, Y. Nordkvelle, & H. Pleasants (Eds.), *Digital storytelling in higher education: International perspectives* (pp. 149-166). Cham, Switzerland: Palgrave Macmillan.

Halberstam, J. (1993). Imagined violence/queer violence: Representation, rage, and resistance. *Social Text, Winter* (37), 187-201.

Hillier, L., Jones, T., Monagle, M., Overton, N., Gahan, L., Blackman, J., & Mitchell, A. (2010). *Writing themselves in 3: The third national study on the sexual health and wellbeing of same sex attracted and gender questioning young people.* Melbourne, Australia: Australian Research Centre in Sex, Health and Society, La Trobe University.

Laverack, G. (2006). Improving health outcomes through community empowerment: A review of the literature. *Journal of Health Population and Nutrition, 24*(1), 113-120. doi:10.3329/jhpn.v24i1.754

Lozano-Neira, N., & Marchbank, J. (2016). Is she one of us? Intersecting identities and social research. *Studies in Qualitative Methodology, 14*(1), 169-190. doi:10.1108/S1042-319220160000014021

Mertens, D. M. (2007). Transformative paradigm. *Journal of Mixed Methods Research, 1*(3), 212-225. doi:10.1177/1558689807302811

Moje, E. B., & MuQaribu, M. (2003). Literacy and sexual identity. *Journal of Adolescent & Adult Literacy, 47*(3), 204-208.

Miller, S. (2015). A queer literacy framework promoting (a)gender and (a)sexuality self-determination and justice. *English Journal, 104*(5), 37-44.

Pennebaker, J. W. (1997). Writing about emotional experiences as a therapeutic process. *Psychological Science, 8*(3), 162-166. doi:10.1111/j.1467-9280.1997.tb00403.x

Rapp Black, E. (2013). *The still point of the turning world.* New York, NY: Penguin Books.

Richardson, L. (2000). Writing: A method of inquiry. In N. Denzin & Y. Lincoln (Eds.), *Handbook of qualitative research* (2nd ed., pp. 923–948). Thousand Oaks, CA: SAGE Publications.

Russon, P. (2017). Beyond trigger warnings: Working towards a strengths-based, trauma-informed model of resilience in the university creative writing workshop. *TEXT, 21*(2), 1-12. Retrieved from http://www.textjournal.com.au/speciss/issue42/Russon.pdf

Strayed, C. (2002, September). The love of my life. *Sun Magazine, 321*. Retrieved from https://www.thesunmagazine.org/issues/321/the-love-of-my-life

Strayed, C. (2012). *Wild: From lost to found on the Pacific Crest Trail.* New York, NY. Alfred A. Knopf.

The Australian Ministerial Council on Education, Employment, Training and Youth Affairs. (2008). *Melbourne declaration on educational goals for young Australians.* Canberra, Australia: MCEETYA.

Tuhiwai Smith, L. (2012). *Decolonizing methodologies: Research and Indigenous peoples* (2nd ed.). London, England: Zed Books.

Vivienne, S. (2016). *Digital identity and everyday activism: Sharing private stories with networked publics.* London, England: Palgrave Macmillan UK.

Wagaman, M. A. (2016). Promoting empowerment among LGBTQ youth: A social justice youth development approach. *Child & Adolescent Social Work Journal, 33*(5), 395-405. doi:10.1007/s10560-016-0435-7

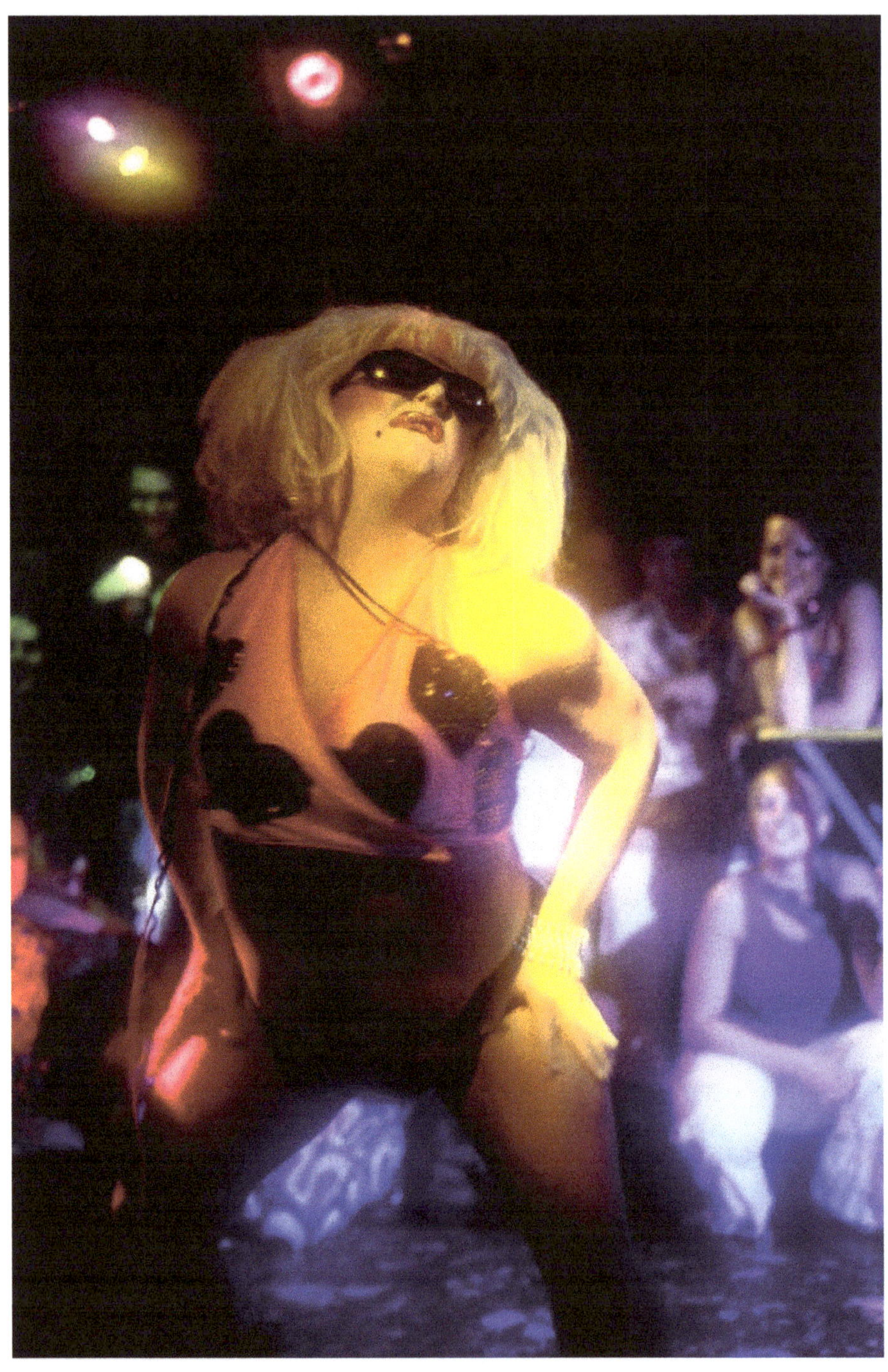

JAMIE JAMES | Vale Lana Turnip, Kooky, Club 77, Darlinghurst, 1996

your voice across the line

Lana you were hanging on the telephone in 1996
but we were all hanging on you

that hair
those lips

hoping you'd rock back your hips
and kiss the nearest queer
leave a cheekful of waxy red they'd see it in the mourning

they'd leave it there for days let hot water
do its quiet work wait
for Sunday wait
to be wrapped in Lana's landline

that beauty spot
those tits

pinkyellowpurpleorangebluegreen light neon nineties for sure
but this could be now this is now

QUINN EADES

Mandy Henningham & Tiffany Jones

Intersex people and internalised corrective bodily bias

Sex essentialism suggests people have an underlying gender 'essence' tied to their sex traits. Doctors can use this essentialist view to medicalise intersex bodies, justify the application of disordering terminologies to these bodies and justify modifying them to fit binary male/ female ideals (Davis, 2015). Doctors may consider an intersex person's genotype, genital appearance, hormones, potential for heteronormative (penis-in-vagina) penetrative sex or fertility to determine their sex marker and plan future interventions. This ignores how any intersex individual's—or anybody's—psychological and social development may contribute to their gender identity (Jones et al., 2016). This chapter aims to explore the quantitative and qualitative findings on gender, sexuality and sexual satisfaction for intersex people to challenge essentialist ideas on bodies. To begin, this chapter will first explore literature on sex, gender and sexuality as it relates to intersex people—defined as people whose sex characteristics (anatomy, hormones or chromosomes) vary from binary male-female sex models. It will then explore sex assignment and gender rearing from birth for participants in an international study of people with intersex variations, followed by whether participants found their reared gender appropriate. It will then inspect the nuances of sexuality and satisfaction, including dating and sexual fantasies.

Sex, gender and sexuality theory and intersex people

Studies of the sex, gender and sexuality of intersex people mainly fall into two schools of thought. The first philosophy is seen in clinical studies trialling interventions on the assumption that bodies should be changed to align with existing sex/ gender models and traditionally heteronormative sexualities (e.g., Ekenze, Nwangwu, Amah, Agugua-obianyo, & Onuh, 2015). There is often a sense of 'concern' in such studies around the 'danger' of lesbianism or homosexuality. In this way, so-called disorders of sex are aligned to past disordering of sexuality. Evaluations of the cases minimise issues of sexual 'dysfunction' (in heterosexual terms) sometimes caused by prioritising sex presentation over pleasure. The second philosophy is seen in both individual intersex authors' narrative studies of their sex/ gender/ sexuality experiences (e.g., Pagonis, 2015) and surveys of intersex participants' views based on the assumption that bodily autonomy is a human right for all individuals (e.g., Jones, 2016). These studies problematized participants' feelings of sexual disconnection, decreased sexual function/pleasure and undesired sex-based presentations where bodily sex 'norm' constructions were imposed upon them from the outside via enforced medical interventions and/ or the gendered expectations of parents.

Butler (1990) argues that there are no pre-existing gendered core identities, and that gender and sexuality are instead performative, a concept that rejects essentialist values. As gender is an act of cultural expectations, this therefore constitutes no universal gender, meaning that all acts of 'women' and 'men' are open to 'resignification'. Butler (1990) goes on to say that sex is subject to a series of social regulations that are directed by law, a form of power; this creates the formative aspects of one's sex as well as gender, pleasures, and desires. This does not mean however that 'anything goes'—one's own desires are experienced in relation to the discourses offered. Gay people may, in heteronormative societies, have fantasies of punishment or forced sex since their 'aberrant' desire for same sex touch cannot be enjoyed without a legitimising excuse (Butler, 1990; Sullivan 2003). Here we consider data from an international survey of people with intersex variations to consider how intersex people engage with essentialist sex, gender and sexuality ideals.

Revisiting an international survey

An anonymous Sydney University Medical School online survey was used to collect data from people with intersex variations, hosted by Survey Monkey. It was piloted by two intersex people. The survey questionnaire contained both forced-choice (quantitative) and open-ended (qualitative) questions. Data were obtained across eleven months (August 2014-June 2015). The recruitment process targeted participants with medically recognised intersex variations who were over the age of 18 and able to discuss their sexuality over time. Processes included online advertisements and emails sent to clinics and health services, and international support organisation newsletters and webpages. Participants needed to self-select to join research. A previous publication considered only participants' healthcare (Henningham & Jones, 2017). Here, we explore the participants' sex, gender and sexuality, using descriptive and comparative statistical analyses undertaken in SPSS and grounded thematic analyses of written responses.

Sex and gender

A total of 81 participants completed the survey, aged from 22 to 71yrs, with a mean age of 43yrs. Participants were from regions including North America (n=47), Europe (n=20), Asia-Pacific (12) and Africa (n=1). They were born in 19 different countries; largely America (n=38), the United Kingdom (n=10), Canada (n=9) and Australia (n=8). The majority of participants were assigned female at birth (54%), fewer were assigned male (39%). The remaining participants were assigned one sex and then reassigned another during their infancy, or were not assigned a sex. Most participants (52%) currently identified as women. Nine expanded with further detail like: *'female probably'*, *'ambiguous female'*, *'neuter/female'*, *'butch female'*, *'female identified, non-binary at times' and 'agender/female'*. A smaller portion of participants identified as men (17%); only one of the men added further ambiguity, stating; '*Male of centre, but I prefer to opt out of gender descriptors*'. Some participants were gender fluid (5%), genderless (4%) and the remainder had a combination of identities. This reflected findings in an Australian study that those assigned male at birth were more likely to have a different gender identity later in life (Jones et al., 2016). In total, almost a third of participants had identities that challenged the two gender binary norms and identified as either fluid or their own subjective interpretation of gender—one participant said, '*gender to me is fluid and playful*'. Another commented that they '*dress in an androgynous attire and love having all the wrong sticky out body parts. I dress as I imagine a hermaphrodite should dress*'.

Gender rearing

Of those participants who were assigned a female sex/ F sex marker, 58% felt the gender they were raised as was appropriate. Conversely, only 23% of those who were assigned male/ M sex marker at birth felt that the gender they were raised as was appropriate; 77% found their gender to be inappropriate. It was statistically significant ($p < 0.05$) that those who were assigned as males at birth and raised as boys were more likely to feel that their gender was inappropriate. This reflected the results of an Australian-only study (Jones et al, 2016). Participants were asked '*how do you feel about the gender you were raised?*'. The most common theme to emerge from this question were participants feeling they did not fit traditional gender roles. Some participants spoke of struggling to fit in with other members of their sex and gender, or feeling like another gender altogether. Others expressed feeling like an outsider, with comments like '*I thought I was an 'it'*' or '*…I was banned from doing things like working out and if I tried out for girls sports I dominated them in a very masculine way, I was called a freak*'. Some participants were punished for not fitting the norms of their gender of rearing, including one who commented, '*I was hit and beat a lot for not acting 'more feminine'*'. Some directly wished they were reared gender neutral. Other others did not mind their sex being assigned but desired to have more choice in their expression of gender: '*I think it is helpful to assign a gender at birth, but the 'door should be left open' allowing the child to develop naturally*'. Participants influenced to enact particular gendered (feminine or masculine) expressions by their parents mostly felt negatively towards their parents. Eighteen participants expressed direct shame; nine expressed anger. Three described feeling left out; one stated, '*it was my body but I couldn't choose anything*'.

Only three participants mentioned feeling happy with their gender rearing. One participant stated that being assigned to be a boy meant he could more easily identify with the gay male community. Another was raised gender neutral,

I picked my clothes from a certain age on, I picked if I wanted a haircut, I asked for my preferred toys. I just had to be a 'girl' in public at school and there I was more one of the boyish girls which was fine, I was not the only one.

This participant discussed that they were directly involved in the decision-making processes for their gender and given agency in determining their presentation and lifestyle, which led to a positive experience overall of being intersex. Another participant expressed that they were accepted for not being completely binary in terms of their activities and interests, '*I tended to be somewhat of a tom boy growing up but that was treated as a normal and acceptable variation of being a girl*'. It was notable that the three participants who were happiest with their gender of rearing were encouraged to be themselves—regardless of the way their sex, gender and sexuality did not strictly align with heterosexual and binary sex 'norms'. This trend towards negative attitudes to rearing that did not foreground the participants' choices reflected other research (Davis, 2015; Jones et al. 2016).

Changing gender

Those participants who changed their gender were asked '*At what age did you begin to think that instead of being the gender you were raised, you should have been another gender?*' A cumulative 71% wanted to be a different gender under the age of 11; the most common age bracket was between 3-5 years old (23%). The responses for a question about the age at which participants decided to affirm another gender, asked only for participants who were currently a different gender to their sex as assigned at birth, yielded diverse answers. In total 37% of participants firmly decided they would change their gender officially at 20+ years of age, followed by 12% firmly wanting to change at 16-19. Three participants stated that they waited to transition or embrace their gender identity out of fear or self-deliberation during their twenties, '*I fought with myself over it throughout my twenties, transitioned at 30*'. Two participants firmly wanted to change gender identity at 11-15 years of age, a further two firmly wanted to change genders at 3-5, and one participant between ages 6-10. When comparing this to the ages of first identifying a need to be a different gender other than the one reared, the majority of firm decisions were made later in life, despite there being signals at an earlier age. However a number of participants noted that concepts of 'transition' often used in participants' discussions were inadequate, '*I cannot transition to herma... Besides, I do not wish to undergo surgery or bodily transformation. I only wish I could get my bod back. But that is impossible*'. These statements illustrated the need for discussing gender change in terms of '*affirmation*' rather than transition; avoiding binary-only models.

Teen dating and sex

Courtship proved to be initially difficult for participants, as a total of 83% of participants stated that they did not feel comfortable dating during their teens. Participants were asked if they were sexually active in their teens. Most (61%) were not. A qualitative investigation of the data revealed a number of themes were reported on the topic. The most common theme around sexual inactivity as a teen was amongst participants were those who did not date in high school (16%). Some participants did not elaborate or give much further detail on this, though some discussed having interests other than sex, '*I had no dates in my teens. I threw myself into sport, and had no sexual awareness*'. Some participants said they actively avoided romantic or sexual encounters due to being intersex. One man said, '*Had one girlfriend in high school, dated a couple of times, kissed and cuddled, but nothing sexual, I was too scared she would find out I wasn't really a boy*'. Three discussed how their avoidance was also because of their sexual orientation, for example one female stated: '*There was no way I was going to be open to a boyfriend or to be sexually active. I was also attracted to girls which confused me more about my sex of rearing and sexual orientation*'. Six participants expressed no interest in sex in high school. One discussed being ridiculed as a result, '*When I was a teenager I had no interest in sex... my sister insisted that I was a homosexual because I showed no interest in sex*'.

In total 39% of participants were sexually active as teens. Seven participants discussed how surgery had made their experiences of sex painful or less pleasurable, for example one woman said '*I was sexually active after vaginoplasty, but didn't tell my male partners. It was very painful*'. Three participants used sex as a means to affirm their gender identity or gain a sense of control; for example one woman said:

I had heard a certain guy was fairly small in size and knew I had a small vagina. Even though I had no interest in him what so ever and he actually repulsed me I felt I had to get this milestone over with to be considered a real girl and not a fake being.

This participant additionally experienced low self-esteem in her teens due to being intersex, and used sex as a replacement for a relationship, '*I started sleeping with anyone who would have me, certain that no one would ever want a relationship with me and that one night stands were the best I could hope for*'. Another participant similarly used sex to affirm her femininity, '*started having sex at 15 in order* TO TRY TO *feel comfortable as a girl, and to prove to them and to me that I* REALLY *was a girl*'. The final participant to emerge in this theme discussed how sex was used not only to validate their gender, but as a method of control over people, '*Sex was validation and control over others. I didn't actually have sex that was good and non-dissociative until decades later, after I transitioned and got new partners who wanted me the way that I actually was*'.

Adult dating and sex

Most participants responding to a question on if they currently had a partner answered 'yes' (64%), whilst just over a third of participants answered 'no'. Participants were asked if they felt comfortable dating in adulthood; more than half (54%) were not comfortable. Fourteen people expressed that they were not comfortable dating because of their body or intersex status, for example one said '*The few occasions where I have been upfront about my intersexuality, the person generally distances themselves from me*'. Three participants felt that it was too complicated and repetitive to explain their intersex variations to people, '*I don't think I would enjoy dating because I would feel a need to explain myself constantly to dates*'. Feeling self-conscious about their physical bodies was also a concern expressed by six participants, for example one said '*It's complicated when your body doesn't represent your gender identity or your sexual orientation*'. Eight participants just felt uncomfortable about sex and not dating, for example one said:

Most people get frustrated to date without having sex and it often feels like I shouldn't bother. It's also been odd to watch people around me be comfortable with one night stands, I would love to be able to do that but I don't feel my body allows that. People looking for one night stands want what they expect.

Only sixteen participants described being comfortable dating. Three said it had been a process to get comfortable, and one commented:

It's often difficult and I've experienced abuse and hate due to being intersex but the connection with others is stronger and more fulfilling than the negative experiences are harmful, so I keep trying to make connections with others.

Trust was crucial to comfort for four participants. One commented, '*I am currently in the longest-term relationship in my life… It took a long time to come to trust this much*'. One participant commented on being part of alternative communities where alternative bodies were more valued; '*I love dating and am out and open about being Intersex, bisexual, pagan, and into the kinky lifestyle*'.

Participants were also directly asked if they experienced enjoyable sex. A total of 71% of those participants who found their reared gender appropriate were reported that they experienced enjoyable sex whereas only 43% of those who found their reared gender inappropriate discussed having enjoyable sex—a statistically significant ($p < 0.04$) difference. Furthermore, participants who were raised as girls were the most likely to go on to experience enjoyable sex (64%) whereas only a third of those reared as boys experienced enjoyable sex. Most participants raised as gender neutral experienced enjoyable sex. Of those who commented on having had unenjoyable sex, pain or discomfort or hindered sensation were dominant themes. For example one said '*The constant bleeding and haemorrhaging and pain (horned retroflexed deformed uterus) during my teens and 20s rather traumatized me about anything connected with the female bits*'. Nine participants also experienced some form of psychological barrier when it came to sex; one said, '*I would love to have my intersex body back and not to feel mutilated. Sometimes I'm also negatively affected by my experiences in sexual situations and become sad*'. One participant said of their partners: '*I end up panicking that the longer they interact with my genitals, the more they'll think I'm a freak*'. Five expressed that they had no interest in sex, another participant talked about only engaging in sex to please their partner.

Of the 24 participants who provided written comments on experiencing enjoyable sex, nine directly mentioned engaging in 'non-heteronormative' sex. Four discussed not having penetrative sex, another discussed feeling too small to penetrate but enjoying other forms of sex, including '*Oral and anal sex as I'm too small to penetrate anything*'. Two genderfluid participants discussed engaging in kink and BDSM (Bondage and Discipline, Sadism and Masochism) play, and one said '*I assume several different roles, different genders, dominant/submissive, penetrative/receptive, etc and I enjoy it immensely*'. Another participant mentioned having '*sex in all kinds of ways with all kinds of bodies*'. Three participants additionally mentioned how being comfortable with themselves allowed them to have improved sex lives, and one noted '*It has gotten better over time*'. Just under half of the participants who had experienced surgical intervention had 'enjoyable sex', whereas most of the participants who had not experienced surgical intervention had 'enjoyable sex'. Only two participants highlighted positive outcomes of surgical intervention for sex: one mentioned being grateful that their vaginoplasty did not result in a loss of sexual sensitivity (though they were self-conscious with new sexual partners); the other said '*aligning my physical sex with my gender made me more confident in approaching people*'.

Sexual fantasies

Participants were asked *'do your sexual fantasies differ from existing experiences?'* Just over half (51%) of the participants stated that their sexual fantasies did not differ from their existing experiences. A further 13% mentioned they did not really experience sexual fantasies, whilst a few fantasised about women, a few fantasised about men and two fantasised about having sex with other intersex people. However, a notable finding of the study was that over a quarter (26%) fantasised about having different genitalia. Four participants discussed fantasising about having a different body altogether including genitalia typical of the sex they fantasised about being. One participant desired having a '*full sized penis*', while another expressed they wanted to be '*normal down there*' for intercourse with their spouse. Several of these individuals described these fantasies in a context of body-shaming and the difficulty of fitting in to current sexual cultures and norms. However, it is important not to conflate these 'different genital' fantasies with a need to pre-emptively change young intersex peoples' bodies in anticipation of these cultures; as some desired body changes were only discovered later in life. For example; one transgender participant expressed the desire for '*typical*' female genitalia; and she explained, '*I have a very strong need to have sex as a female with the right parts*' as she grew older.

Moreover, several bisexual participants discussed fantasising about having different genitalia when having sex with people of different sexes in inconsistent ways throughout life. One married bisexual woman explained:

I often fantasise that I have a penis and am having sex with a woman/women. I don't think this necessarily means anything except that I'm very much bisexual and miss having sex with women!

There were two male participants who reported fantasies about being a woman in a heterosexual relationship, '*I have always envisaged myself as a female in a hetero relationship but, the older I get, the less significant that is*'. Further, some participants discussed fantasising about having their surgically unaltered bodies back. One said, '*I fantasize about what my life would have been like without genital surgery or having my breasts removed. I can't seem to get excited thinking about anything else, really*'. One participant fantasised about having both sets of typical genitals, stating '*I do fantasize about have a full set of both genitals. I sort of don't have either*'. Fantasies thus played with notions of typicality in atypical combinations and queer, inconsistent scenarios. The fantasies mostly reinforced the need for individuals to retain their own anatomy where possible and their own autonomy around bodily choices, whilst showing that internalisation of sex-gender norms sometimes affected how they understood their desires.

Conclusion

Intersex people expressed a broad spectrum of sexual behaviours and fantasies in this study. Many engaged in pleasurable non-heteronormative sex. However, most treatments and gender rearing practices they were exposed to prepared them for lives in a heteronormative binary society demanding penis-in-vagina sex. These data suggested such essentialist models of sex, gender, and sexuality *may not fit* intersex peoples' experiences. They suggested the importance of allowing intersex people room for personal expression and choice, regardless of the sex marker applied in their early years (although female and gender neutral markers and rearing may allow more flexibility). Further, these data suggested that some intersex people fantasise about having different bodies due to shame and cultural oppression—as internalised homophobia can stimulate punishment fantasies (Sullivan, 2003). As the 'corrective bias' over intersex bodies appears internalised here, a proposed term for further research is 'internalised corrective bodily bias'; describing the disconnection between some intersex peoples' bodies and fantasised sexual selves. It also captures how bisexual intersex participants sometimes 'corrected' their *imagined bodies* in otherwise same sex fantasises, to maintain 'heteronormativity'. This bias may also played out when intersex people refrain from desired dating or sexual experiences; or engage in *undesired* sex. Internalised corrective bodily bias appeared associated with rigidly gendered rearing. Thus, enforcing strict relations between sex markers assigned at birth, bodies and gender expression to maintain gender essentialist myths can be psychologically (and physically) scarring. Medical and familial supports operating from more flexible gender theories could better support intersex peoples' future sexual experiences and lessen their dating anxiety.

References

Butler, J. (1990). *Gender trouble: Feminism and the subversion of identity.* London: Routledge.

Davis, G. (2015). *Contesting Intersex: The Dubious Diagnosis.* New york: NYU Press.

Ekenze, S., Nwangwu, E., Amah, C., Agugua-obianyo, N., & Onuh, A. (2015). Disorders of sex development in a developing country. *Pediatric Surgery International,, 31*(1), 93-99.

Henningham, M., & Jones, T. (2017). Cut it Out: Rethinking Surgical Intervention on Intersex Infants. In T. Jones (Ed.), *Bent Street.* (pp. 55-67). Melbourne: Clouds of Magellan.

Jones, T. (2016). The Needs of Students with Intersex Variations. *Sex Education,, 16*(6), 602-618. Retrieved from http://www.tandfonline.com/doi/abs/10.1080/14681811.2016.1149808?journalCode=csed20

Jones, T., Hart, B., Carpenter, M., Ansara, G., Leonard, W., & Lucke, J. (2016). *Intersex: Stories and Statistics from Australia.* London: Open Book Publisher.

Pagonis, P. (2015). The Son They Never Had. *Narrative Inquiry in Bioethics,, 5*(2), 103-106.

Michael Bernard Kelly

Love's Pure Light

A Reflections on the Passage of Marriage Equality

Marriage Equality was passed by the Australian Parliament on December 7, 2017. The following speech was delivered by Michael Kelly at the Sydney Town Hall on December 24, 2017, as part of the annual Christmas Eve Service presented by the Metropolitan Community Churches (MCC) in Sydney. For over two decades MCC has offered this service of carols and readings as a gift to the city's LGBTIQ communities, and to the people of Sydney.

Joy to the world! What a wondrous, grace-filled evening this is, as we gather together on this extraordinary Christmas Eve—a Christmas Eve that is, for us here Australia, one like no other!

It is a great honour and a true delight to be invited to be with you tonight, and to be asked to find some words, some reflections, some hints of insight into all that is stirring in our hearts and minds, in our souls and our bodies—and in the heart of our community—on this unique Christmas Eve.

I am very grateful to the people of MCC Sydney for inviting me to join you tonight—but then, each one of us is here in response to an invitation. Yes, an invitation from MCC, who have faithfully opened their doors and their community for some 22 Christmas Eves—but there is a deeper invitation—often barely glimpsed, deep in our spirits, that draws us here—perhaps in spite of ourselves, in spite of the endless distractions and diversions thrown at us in great cities like this—and in spite of the cynicism that contemporary societies so often evoke and promote.

What is it that has stirred within us tonight, and drawn us out of our homes, away from parties and shopping, from dinner and drinks, and even empowered us to navigate our way around the endless construction on George Street—to gather here and listen to ancient readings, sing old carols, share communion and listen to a gay theologian?

All around the world tonight, at midnight, millions of people of every race and gender and class will hear these words from a long-dead Jewish prophet: 'The People that walked in darkness has seen a Great Light. On those who walked in a land of deep shadow, a Light has shone!'

All of us, each one of us, is here tonight because somewhere, somehow, sometime, we have, in our lives as LGBTIQ people, seen, however tentatively, Great Light! It is that seeing, that Light, that has drawn us here tonight. We come seeking to share that Light, to celebrate that Light, to be blessed again and again by that Light.

And yet, in the midst of this gathering, it is important to recognize that over these past few months, as we have endured the national debate about Marriage Equality, far too many of us LGBTIQ Australians have found old experiences of walking in darkness coming back to haunt us. There have been times when we felt, once again, that ours was a land where we had to walk in deep shadow—the shadow of oppression, judgment, exclusion, condemnation. For all of us, and especially those of a certain age, like me, this experience evoked visceral memories of darkness—both personal and communal—that we once thought would never give way to light.

I'd invite us all to take a moment, to be still, and to go within. Let's close our eyes, slow down our breathing, feel our bodies sitting in this room in the heart of Sydney, and allow the noise of the city outside to fall away. Let's all take a moment of silence together …

In the secrecy of your own heart, I invite you to remember your own experience of walking in darkness: a darkness within, where hope seemed impossible; darkness without, where the communities that claimed to love you demanded, however subtly, the sacrifice of the deepest longings of your heart and your body. Remember how it felt to walk in that darkness. We've all had moments of deep darkness—dare to taste yours once again. Remember that people all around the world, tonight, still walk in such darkness.

Now I invite each of us to become deeply present to that moment when you first began to glimpse, however tentatively, the fragile, hint of light—the first dawning of the possibility that being who you are, desiring how you desire, loving how you love—might just, perhaps, be ok—might even, maybe, be good.

Feel again that moment. How did it come? In a conversation? During prayer? While reading a book? While watching a movie? Was it at a time of desperation and hopelessness? Was it during love-making and sexual play? Did it come through someone else—whose kind word or soft touch or tentative kiss somehow brought a gentle, tender light into your land of deep shadow?

Sit with that light for a moment. Feel again the first breath of hope, of freedom, of quiet joy that it brought—that first hint of light in your darkness. Holy Light. Love's pure light. Light that liberates and heals and empowers. Sometimes very tentative, but ultimately irresistible. Light that has stayed with you all these years—and that has brought you—us—here tonight. The people that walked in darkness have indeed seen Great Light!

Sometimes the Light breaks through with passion and clarity, in one transforming moment—sometimes it is gentle and it grows quietly and steadily stronger and more radiant—often over many years. And yet, however it may have dawned in our individual lives, all of us are here tonight because we, in our own darkness, have seen, and trusted in, Great Light.

Over the past twenty years I have been reflecting on the ways our spiritual and sexual journeys interweave and inform, enrich and transform each other. This has involved some in-depth spiritual interviews with, in particular, gay men. A few years ago, as part of my doctoral research, I interviewed a man I will call David. I would like to read a brief excerpt from that interview for you.

David had grown up in a rigidly repressed Irish Catholic family. He had struggled for years to crush any hint of desire or passion or sexual feeling. One evening, while still a young man, he was gently drawn into love-making by another man. I said to David: So this was the first time you had ever …

David: Ever touched a man. Let alone touched every part of his body!

Me: And he yours

David: And he mine. He loved my body—which was beyond comprehension—how did that happen?

Me: How was that for you? We've talked about some pretty dark and deep things and long periods of depression and repression …

David: It's astounding—I received it so happily and graciously—and as I look back, I didn't feel guilt or shame about it …

Me: So, what did you feel?

David: I felt—alive! I felt seen and known and desired and free to do exactly carnally what I wanted to do. And I was amazed that I knew everything I wanted to do—it was all there, it was all present, and it was coming out with joy and passion and noise and…. I felt totally alive in it and loved it… I was alive, I felt totally alive, I felt totally integrated—that word is even too intellectual—I felt totally me. I felt totally like a creature of God—there were no little parts on the edges that were feeling unwelcome …

'The Light shines in the darkness'. 'The Word was made flesh'. 'I came that you may have life, and have it to the full!' So often these words of Scripture are taken to refer only to some sort of inner spiritual realm, some rather ethereal, other-worldly kind of reality, or they are applied to a claim that somehow God saves us in spite of our murkiness and ineradicable sin.

Tonight I want to say that the Light shines, the Word is made flesh within and through and as US—in our flesh and in our concrete, real, sweaty, messy, realities—and that wherever a person is being freed to be themselves, to touch and be touched with reverence and passion, to feel their humanness, to delight in the goodness of their body, to dare to imagine a life that brings joy and freedom into their hearts, there—in that place and person—Christ is being born, Divine Love is becoming flesh, salvation is being made real. This is the Incarnation, this is the message of Christmas.

At the same time, this inner birth, for all its power and wonder, is not simply a personal and private liberation—it also happens in the concrete realities of our time and our culture. There is one Light, one radiance, and it shines in and for everyone. David, whose words I have just quoted, went on to live a long life of dedicated service, through the worst of the AIDS epidemic, and in his late sixties he is still helping others to find health and inner freedom. This dawning of light is transformative in the deepest sense—and it spreads out into the world and into the communities around us—and everyone here tonight, I believe, has sensed this light and tasted this transformation. We LGBTIQ people have known many people in our lives and in communities who have broken through personal and communal darkness and who have then gone on to pour out their lives in shining, radiant service and love.

A great Christian mystic once wrote: 'What good is it to me that Mary gave birth to the Son of God hundreds of years ago, if I do not also give birth to the Son of God in my time and in my culture? We are all meant to be mothers of God. God is always needing to be born'.

These words can be a bracing corrective to the sentimentality that often saturates Christmas. They are also a corrective to the cynicism we can sometimes feel—another Christmas with endless carols on a music-loop, in every department store and every elevator! Another December with the implicit demand that we get excited—again—about a feast most of us have celebrated for more years than we care to number!

What this mystic—Meister Eckhart—is saying tonight, right here in Sydney, on this Christmas Eve, is this: 'Tell me about the Holy Birth within YOU! How did YOU first begin to sense the birth of light and freedom and love within your actual life—and—how are you bringing that same light and love and freedom to birth in your community and your society?

This Holy Birth is not only about expanding our individual hearts and bringing us personal freedom and joy and a new and deeper kind of breathing—it is also empowers us to live in the world in such a way that we re-make it. In such a way that we re-make it.

And re-make it we have.

I began this talk by asking us to do some reflection on our personal experience of light shining in the darkness. Our society, too, has walked in darkness and the shadow of death—many of us here tonight have experienced that first hand. And yet, in the space of half a lifetime we have transformed Australia from a place where poofters and perverts were to be bashed or jailed, to a society that overwhelmingly affirms that not only are our relationships to be tolerated, they are to be celebrated and honoured! WE have done this—it didn't happen through some kind of societal or spiritual osmosis—it happened through us living and loving with courage and passion and freedom and honesty, through our persistent refusal to be consigned to walk in darkness and the shadow of death. It happened through 22 years of Christmas Eve services like this.

We have brought this holy light to birth in our world, in our time and in our culture.

This is the Incarnation! This is Divine Love becoming flesh in us and in our society. This is the radiance of Love's pure light—as the carol so beautifully puts it. This love not only re-creates individual hearts, it critiques, challenges, and changes social, cultural and political structures. As this love is born, again, in our time, the concrete realities of our world become permeable to the transforming possibility of justice, freedom, compassion, and radical inclusion. And this love always gathers with particular intensity around those who have been, in any age, consigned to the shadows and the margins. For, ultimately, no one and no situation, nothing that exists, nothing still to come, is excluded from the embrace of the One whose name is Love.

And here, we encounter Mystery. For yes, the birth of the Light is about each of us and our human communities and the path towards freedom, love and transformation—and yet, none of this can begin to exhaust the wonder, the grace, the inexpressible immensity of the embrace we celebrate tonight. Heaven and earth meet here and kiss—God embraces matter, flesh, creation, the entire cosmos, in the heart of that little baby.

In the wonder of Christmas we are caught up in something that reaches into the deepest parts of ourselves—and that is also beyond us and our individual and communal struggles. This is of God. This is the Love that moves the sun and the stars. What can we say of it?

All of our words are only stammering responses to the mystery of God from God, Light from Light, true God from true God, breathing in the tiny body of the Babe of Bethlehem—and, in a very real sense, in every baby.

If we cannot find words for the mystery itself, can we say something of what the Christmas message might mean for human living and loving? The Babe of Bethlehem, after all, was not just divine, cosmic love become human, he was born into a very real community and into a very troubled century. One theologian who has attempted to offer an example of what it means when divine love becomes human is James Alison, who is a gay theologian from the UK.

Alison says that in the Mystery of the Incarnation, in Christmas, it's as if God's love became a pebble of light, which was dropped into the vast dark pond of human experience. This little pebble of light, of liberation, of love without limit, without containment, without exclusion, sends out ripples of love and light all across the waters and over the centuries, embracing everything and everyone. In every age and in every culture these ripples of love wash up against a barrier, a boundary, a border, which was constructed by us humans to keep some people in and some people out. So often we call these barriers 'sacred'—and yet the ripples of love gently, inexorably wash them away.

As the ripples of love and light continue to spread out, embracing more and more of the human experience, they reach, in every age, a new barrier. There is, again and again, a pitched battle as some people proclaim, 'this is the do or die moment—this is the last battle for all that is holy!' and they frantically strive to shore up the sad little barriers that they think protect themselves and all that is sacred.

We have endured just such a battle in these past few months, as the protectors of the sacred barriers have sought to beat back the waves of equality and love and inclusion. How hard they struggled!

And yet, the waves of God's irresistible love gently but surely ripple outwards like ever-embracing arms, and they erode and dissolve and wash away all the 'sacred barriers', including our own, and we discover that love is more wondrously vast, more gently powerful, and more utterly inclusive than we could ever have imagined.

Of course, all this does not happen by magic—but it does happen through grace, the grace embodied in our own lives and in our longing to live with integrity and freedom and to empower others to do the same.

Our celebrations this month, and here tonight, are all about the rippling out of this eternal, uncontainable love. We see this, we embrace this, and we rejoice! However, even in the midst of our joy, our relief and our delight, these celebrations will be ultimately empty if we are not aware of the barriers, exclusions and borders still waiting to be dissolved by love.

We are called, as ever, to be aware of all those who are still forced to walk in darkness and deep shadow, in the many ways this continues to happen in our society and around the world. This is the never-ending work of the Incarnation and the true meaning of Christmas—the call to welcome the stranger, to feed the hungry, to free the captives, to shelter the homeless, to care for the earth and her creatures.

We know—you and I—what it is to walk in a land of deep shadow. We know what it is to see Great Light. May our living, our loving, our divine incarnations, ever more freely and more passionately, bring light and radiance to every last corner of our world.

Tiffany Jones

2018—the year in queer: refusal tweets

The status quo can use social pressure to gain the conforming erasure of minority groups. Refusing to relieve this tension—*not* conforming to normalising pressure—defies their expectations. A refusal constitutes practices primarising strength in affirmation of self, or a group's representation, despite normalising pressure. Refusing to comply with normalising pressure thus complicates power dynamics and bully/victim binaries in useful ways. This article offers Queer analysis of refusals to relieve tension in 2018. It is organised by Tweets linked to notable refusals in each month of the year.

JANUARY

Hayley Kiyoko

@HayleyKiyoko, #20GAYTEEN, #expectations2018. Hayley Kiyoko (Japanese European American Singer Director Actor Dancer) is a former Disney star nicknamed the 'Lesbian Jesus' by her LGBTIQ+ youth fan-base. In January 2018 Kiyoko pushed positive representation through initiating the *#20gayteen* movement via her Twitter and other social media, in which LGBTIQ+ youth created memes celebrating small positive experiences of being queer in their everyday lives. The year-specific movement counters the victimisation associated with queer teenagers in research and the media (Copland & Rasmussen, 2017; Jones, 2013). Kiyoko's mainstream music videos feature bold multi-cultural and sensual queer content enhancing this affirmative representation. In these clips she repeatedly plays a girl with 'swagger' who often 'gets the girl' in a subversion of heterosexual music videos, and her fans' response echoes the queer celebration of Madonna's subversion of gendered music video roles (Railton & Watson, 2011, p. 4). Kiyoko's works transfer Queer music video strategies into mainstream pop music videos including irony, camp, parody, pastiche and mimesis (Hawkins, 2016; Leibetseder, 2016). Her works refuse fairy-tale marriage-like resolutions to the relationships explored—the sexual engagements depicted are intense, unclear and unfinished in a manner which speaks to youth experiences. However, the queer protagonist always refuses victimisation for affirming alternatives.

FEBRUARY

Adam Rippon

@Adaripp. Adam Rippon, figure-skater and Olympian represented the USA at the February 2018 Winter Olympic Games in Seoul South Korea. Asked by the media whether he would meet with Vice President Mike Pence at the Winter Games, Rippon had apparently responded with a refusal:

> *I would absolutely not go out of my way to meet somebody who I felt has gone out of their way to not only show that they aren't a friend of a gay person but that they think that they're sick* (Leah, 2018).

This refusal, carried through onto his social media including a series of Tweets, created significant media debate and backlash around the world. It disrupted the expectation that a gay Olympian should act honoured to meet with a political leader regardless of their homophobic policy record. It disrupted the idea that the publicity opportunities surrounding Olympic events should be prioritised over everyday concerns. Rippon used the interview to instead draw attention to Pence's funding of gay conversion therapy and efforts to support exemptions for discrimination on the basis of sexual orientation and gender identity. He repeatedly refused to meet with, or engage in subsequent offers of photo opportunities with, Pence towards diffusing the tension (Leah, 2018). Other Olympians including freestyle skier Gus Kenworthy also spoke out against Pence and released tweets throughout the games like '*We're here. We're queer. Get used to it*' (Belam, 2018).

MARCH

Emma Gonzalez

@Emma4Change. Emma Gonzalez, a Cuban-American school student and *March For Our Lives* Campaign Co-founder, was a survivor of the 2018 USA Parkland School shooting earlier in the year. She was part of a cohort of students who inspired people of younger ages to raise their voice and advocate for gun control, in a youth-based gun control movement responding to shootings young people experienced in American schools, public and private settings (Reilly, 2018). The movement has been characterised by large-scale youth marches and rallies, meetings with politicians and leaders of gun interest groups and mass everyday youth and shooting victim networks' involvement—including through Twitter and other social media. The movement is particularly notable for the way it has featured young people directly drawing strong attention in their speeches and meetings to the inactivity of politicians. They argue this inactivity is influenced by the increased investments of the National Rifle Association (NRA) into American politicians. March for Our Lives has incited extreme backlash from some politicians and interest groups, who attacked Emma on the basis of her shaved head and open bisexuality, or tried to suggest she and other youth in the movement were 'crisis actors'—adults pretending to be child victims of crises. Emma Gonzalez queers the expectations of her age and her activism. In one 'speech', she subverted the generic expectations that she would speak in detail about her story for the audience—standing in silence for six minutes (Reilly, 2018). This act created a long unrelieved tension to highlight the amount of time it took for 17 students' lives to be taken by gun violence at her school earlier in the year, 15 more injured and many others permanently changed.

APRIL

IHRA

@intersexaus. Intersex Human Rights Australia (IHRA) an independent not-for-profit organisation promoting the development of supports for by and for people with intersex variations or traits, changed its name in April 2018 (from Organisation Intersex International/ OII Australia). However, it did not change and has refused to change its core issue, expressed by its social media. The organisation's work over the past decade has focused on human rights, bodily autonomy and self-determination, and on promoting the development of 'evidence-based, patient-directed healthcare' (Intersex Human Rights Australia, 2018). They received no public funds and up until December 2016, the organisation was volunteer-run; since that date they have two part-time co-executive directors. Whilst the organisation has contributed to Australian Parliamentary inquiries into discrimination laws and enforced and coerced sterilisation procedures impacting its focal community (OII Australia, 2012, 2013), and works closely alongside other Australian and international organisations with different foci, it does not let direct intersex representation and activism be lost within contributions to broader LGBTIQ+ and disability movements. Co-executive Director Morgan Carpenter released a paper commenting on this refusal of Australian intersex action to be erased by intersectional work whilst the core issues for people with intersex variations—'normalization' of intersex bodies and 'othering' of intersex identities—remain:

> *The existence of intersex has also been instrumentalized for the benefit of other, intersecting, populations. (…) Australian attempts at reforms to recognize the rights of intersex people have either failed to adequately comprehend the population affected or lacked implementation. An emerging human rights consensus demands an end to social prejudice, stigma, and forced medical interventions,*

focusing on the right to bodily integrity and principles of self-determination (Carpenter, 2018, p. 1).

The work to ensure these goals is multifarious and ongoing.

MAY

Sonia Correa

@ips_journal. Brazilian researcher Sonia Correa is Director of Sexual Policy Watch (SPW), a project based at the Brazilian organisation ABIA (National AIDS Policy Watch). She warned LGBTIQ, gender studies and feminist thinkers in May via media and social media that European and Latin-American Anti-Gender Movements promoting essentialist views of sex were increasing their alliance (Correa, 2018). Recalling the vicious physical attack on Queer theorists and post-structuralist feminists Judith Butler and Wendy Brown at a Rio de Janiero Airport at the end of 2017 on the basis of their work on gender, Correa described how the conservative movement against 'gender ideology' had not only since worsened in Brazil, but become increasingly globalised (Correa, 2018). This phenomenon of global conservative networking has in the past particularly impacted transgender student rights and marriage equality pushes and been spurred on by Russian and US alt-right incitement and funding (Jones, 2016). Correa commented:

> *...anti 'gender ideology' crusades are neither a novelty nor exclusively Latin American. Moreover, the semantic frame 'gender ideology' reveals itself as an empty and adaptable signifier, encompassing a broad range of demands such as the right to abortion, sexual orientation and gender identity, to diverse families, education in gender and sexuality, HIV prevention and sex work, a basic basket that can be easily adjusted to the conditions of each context. Its discourses construct unusual analogies between feminism, queer theory and communism, a strategy that has echoes in contexts where this spectrum remains active, such as Brazil. Above all, anti-gender proponents mobilise simplistic logic and imaginaries and constitute volatile enemies—here the feminists, there the gays, over there the artists,*

ahead the academics, elsewhere the trans bodies—nourishing moral panics that distract societies from structural issues that they should be debating, such as growing inequalities of gender, class, race and ethnicity. Although they use theological arguments, anti-gender campaigns speak the language of the Planet Animal (Correa, 2018).

Correa and SPW refuse to pretend gender and sexuality are other than plastic, unstable constructions and have been highlighting the coalitions aimed at sustaining that pretence (Correa, 2018). They call for long-term work that counters the anti-rights work of transnational gender ideology networks.

JUNE

Hannah Gadsby

@Hannahgadsby. Hannah Gadsby, an Australian Comedian and Star of the Netflix Show 'Nanette', decided to quit comedy this year. As she explained throughout her intended last leg of her intended last US tour of her stand-up show 'Nanette' and her social media (Gadsby, 2018), Gadsby was tired of telling jokes about her own experiences of homophobia with punchlines that stopped her story short of its dénouement where she was in reality repeatedly punched—and felt so deserving she didn't seek medical help. She was tired of enacting a humility about her gender expression on stage to make it less awkward for mainstream comedy audiences that felt more like enacting a humiliation, and re-enacting it and re-enacting it over and over until it compounded with a life-time of off-stage humiliations. She was tired of the comedic genre's standard cycle of building and relieving tension about being too female, being not female enough, being too lesbian, being not lesbian enough… of the expectation she must relieve tension about 'being'. A major trope of comedic writing is the regular relieving of tension after 'a relatively short amount of time'; indeed relieving comedy is seen as a 'must' in order to gain the redemptive positive moment of laughter to otherwise negative anecdotes (Heller, 2005, p. 75). Gadsby stopped relieving the tension in her show (Gadsby, 2018). She used the power of her personal stories' endings to enhance tension to its utmost point. She turned that tension back on audience members, responding to the zeitgeist in which she felt situated including the #MeToo Movement—which has seen people call out sexually abusive predators, sexually abusive workplaces and sexually abusive industries. Gadsby's show called out comedy. When 'Nanette' aired on Netflix; it was received as a watershed moment in not only comedy, but in the #MeToo Movement; in narratives of art history; and in the cultural depiction of LGBTIQ+ people. Instead of quitting comedy, Gadsby 'queered' it by refusing its heteronormative structures and regressive expectations of the tension of 'requisite woman hating' (Jagose, 1996, p. 53), and inhabiting her stage more fully as a person outside gender and sexual norms without maintaining that non-normativity as 'funny'.

JULY

Stella Nyanzi

Stella Nyanzi, Ugandan LGBTIQ+ Rights Ally & Womens Lives Matter Campaigner, refused to be drawn into easy arguments for or against LGBTIQ+ peoples' religious freedoms in Ugandan media debates across July. That month a Youtube video had surfaced of missing former Ugandan LGBTIQ+ activist Val Kalende, who had experienced extreme difficulties finding work and significant isolation after seeking asylum in Canada. The film depicted Val Kalende now back in Uganda wearing uncharacteristic gender conforming clothes, kneeling before an evangelical Christian pastor and (a sometimes jeering) church community and renouncing LGBTIQ activism and lesbian activity. In the video Val speaks of the isolation suffered after having been orphaned by the past rejections of family and community. Clearly, returning to Uganda *after achieving Canadian asylum*—which Kalende had called a difficult process due to Canada's requirement of LGBTIQ+ 'credibility' (for example letters of confirmation from ex-girlfriends)—was complicated. Particularly *given the murders* of Kalende's past Ugandan LGBTIQ+ activists friends. Nyanzi refused to be baited into making points about Kalende's sexuality or the genuineness of her individual experience of religion in her effort to seek safety and community in Uganda. She commented instead on the possibility of a refusal of religious shame. Nyanzi's refusal to join in a media or community beat-up of people who assert varying identity formations over time denaturalises 'stable identity' (Butler, 2004) in Queer and compassionate ways; and focusses more on seeking 'liveability' than holding people to identity stability.

AUGUST

Pussy Riot

@pussyriot. Pussy Riot, a Russian punk band, is known for creating political protest music about points of tension in Russian culture including LGBTIQ rights, freedom of speech and feminist themes. The band's bold public performances and protests have led to the arrest of various members; and their being declared '*a common enemy*' of ethno-religious traditionalism in Russian sociology (Dugin, 2014, p.169). In 2018 they released a new song 'Unicorn Freedom', promoting the song through an August Tweet from the group's Twitter and Youtube accounts explaining unicorns as a symbol of protest in Russia, which has featured in Russian propaganda against LGBTIQ people in Western countries (US House of Representatives Democrats Permanent Selection Committee on Intelligence, 2018). The electronic track is dedicated to Anya Pavlikova, a girl aged only 17 years old when she was arrested in her bedroom; a space decorated in unicorn posters. She faced the potential of 10 years in a Russian prison for participating in a teen girl 'Telegram chat group' that used to meet at McDonalds to discuss 'boys, exams and politics' and was at times critical of Putin (Arcand, 2018). The song highlighted the absurdity of a girl being cast as an enemy of the state in a Russian domestic intelligence sting operation through its use of overplay—an over-the-top use of stereotypical gender iconography (Bredbeck, 2002). In 'Unicorn Freedom' the overplay specifically focusses on a childish girlishness; the song is an overly sweet-sounding bubble-gum techo tune recorded in a high-pitched, soft and 'sing-song' light Russian female voice. The music video features a pastel pink background and mesmerising array of unicorns, seals, kittens, bunnies and rainbows float dreamily—recalling Queer camp (in Leibetseder, 2016, p.59). Throughout the track the unicorn emoji symbol next to the words 'UNICORN FREEDOM' continually drifts across the screen, mimicking a screen-saver for an online group chat. Choruses punctuated by a child's giggle warn the police to better treat girls using the unicorn: '*Hey cop don't put us in prison, the unicorn's here to protect us*'. The techno beat increases with a fast overlay of unicorn symbols, suggesting increased protest.

SEPTEMBER

Evie Macdonald

Evie Macdonald, a thirteen year old Australian school girl, refused to accept what she framed as a transphobic Tweet by her newly minted Australian Prime Minister Scott Morrison. In September 2018, she pre-filmed and submitted her comment for a segment on the Australian television program '*The Project*' on which the Prime Minister was set to appear. She responded to his tweeted comment on a *Daily Telegraph* article which made incorrect claims about how gender issues are dealt with in schools—suggesting teachers were trained to identify potential transgender children. Morrison tweeted the misleading article with the comment that: '*We do not need 'gender whisperers' in our schools. Let kids be kids*'. In her film clip response Evie Macdonald addressed the politician directly, stating:

> *My name is Evie Macdonald, I'm thirteen years old and I'm a transgender kid, and this is what I want to say to the Prime Minister. There are thousands of kids in Australia that are gender diverse and we don't deserve to be disrespected like that through tweets from our Prime Minister. I know what it's like to be on the receiving end of attitudes like this. I went to a Christian school where I had to pretend*

to be a boy and spend weeks in conversion therapy. We get one childhood and mine was stolen from me by attitudes like this (Tenplay, 2018).

Morrison, when asked what he had to say to Macdonald, appeared to back-pedal on his earlier comments with: '*Well, I love all Australians and whatever background they come from*' (Tenplay, 2018). Evie Macdonald's appearance had disrupted Morrison's argument, showing that where schools do enforce gender policies on unwilling, these can actually be conservative Christian gender-tropes. Macdonald had previously spoken out in the media when it was attacking the Safe Schools Coalition program which had helped her talk to her principal about her needs (Alcorn, 2016). She had also given speeches about how helpful resources like the book '*The Gender Fairy*' would have been to her when she was younger, when it received negative media attention (Hirst, 2018). Macdonald's speeches and interviews refused to let powerful figureheads speak about transgender youth, without transgender youth.

OCTOBER

Bill Shorten

@billshortenmp. Bill Shorten, Leader of the Australian Labor Party, has repeatedly refused to let any of the nation's recent Australian-Prime-Minister-des-Jours (alternately Tony Abbott, Malcom Turnbull and Scott Morrison) rest on LGBTI rights. In his role as Leader of the Opposition, key strategies included to capitalise on the (various) Prime Ministers' promises for debates, to push for genuine progress by publicly and repeatedly holding them to their promises. Regardless of the political gains this certainly brings Labor it has been of undeniable value to growing the *direct textual recognition* of LGBTI peoples' rights in Australian legislation. This strategy has been used by Shorten and other members of his party particularly including Tanya Plibersek on issues including discrimination law (Koziol, 2018; Shorten, 2018); marriage rights (Griffiths, 2015); and Safe Schools (Medhora,

2016). In October, the Prime Minister Scott Morrison pledged to abolish religious schools' right to expel LGBT students as a matter of urgency, after the issue came to public attention as part of the leaked recommendations of Philip Ruddock's religious freedom review. Shorten wrote a letter to Prime Minister Scott Morrison offering to support his promise. Shorten refused to let Morrison forget the promise, or the nation. Shorten tweeted about the promise sharing his letter to the PM, starting in October and then repeatedly. On December 2nd 2018 Bill Shorten introduced legislation on it into the Lower House of Parliament (Shorten, 2018), and pushed alongside Tanya Plibersek for its fair debate (Koziol, 2018).

NOVEMBER

Twitter

Twitter Rules and Policies (Twitter, 2018), a document managed and regularly updated online, changed in November to become more inclusive of LGBTI people. November is a month associated with transgender days of remembrance, rights protests and social contribution celebration in many parts of the world and particularly the US where Twitter, Inc. is based. In November 2018 Twitter responded to the increased activism by transgender people who had been misgendered using the social media format both preceding and during the month, the surge in complaints from transgender users, and various research reports by updating its terms of service to offer greater protection. Any user who deliberately targets a trans person (or people) with abuse including misgendering and deadnaming may now be reported and banned from the platform according to the *Hateful Conduct* Policy (Twitter, 2018):

> *You may not promote violence against or directly attack or threaten other people on the basis of race, ethnicity, national origin, sexual orientation, gender, gender identity, religious affiliation, age, disability, or serious disease. (…)Research has shown that some groups of people are disproportionately targeted with abuse online. This includes;*

women, people of color, lesbian, gay, bisexual, transgender, queer, intersex, asexual individuals, marginalized and historically underrepresented communities. For those who identity with multiple underrepresented groups, abuse may be more common, more severe in nature and have a higher impact on those targeted.

Explaining that bans may occur over repeated and/ or non-consensual slurs, the policy now explains this ground *'includes targeted misgendering or deadnaming of transgender individuals'*. The Twitter policy text refused use of incorrect names (a former name no longer used can be considered a 'dead name') or pronouns to degrade transgender people.

DECEMBER

Penny Wong

@SenatorWong. Senator Penny Wong, Australian Labor Party Leader of the Opposition in the Senate, refused to accept delays to Prime Minister Scott Morrison's promised removal of exemptions in the Sex Discrimination Act allowing religious schools to discriminate against staff and students on the basis of gender and sexual orientation. The Senate Legal and Constitutional Affairs Committee had recommended that the Australian Government act to remove the exemptions (Recommendation 3, 2.131), based on a range of submissions from a November inquiry into how the exemptions impacted students, teachers and school communities (Australian Parliament Senate Legal and Constitutional Affairs Committee, 2018). When the Morrison Administration moved to push back the debate over the legislation to January 2019, Senator Penny Wong joined a range of politicians from diverse parties in pressuring the Prime Minister to make good on his promise to stop allowing LGBT kids to be expelled from Australian schools by removing the exemptions. Senator Wong stands out in Australian politics for her cross-party collaborations; understanding that her own refusals of discrimination are even stronger voiced alongside those of politicians across the bench. She understands that uplifting 'unexpected' refusals of the delay—

such as she did when re-tweeting a refusal from a NSW Nationals MP like Trevor Khan—can be more subversive than authoring her own refusal in an oppositional leadership role and as Australia's first openly out lesbian senator. Wong is celebrated for her collaborative approach of uplifting others' voices and changing others' minds:

> *Senate Opposition Leader Penny Wong is what we should seek in a lawmaker—experienced, principled, collaborative. She is steely but not uncompromising. A lesbian who accepted but did not agree with her party's previous opposition to marriage equality, she fought internally to change the policy and emerged as one of the most respected, respectful and convincing advocates for ending that injustice. She fought beautifully for her family (…) Penny Wong is one of the best leaders in contemporary Australian history (Short, 2017).*

Conclusion

Refusal of dominant gender and sexuality expectations or responding with Queer strategies to other imposed expectations is a relatively risky Queer approach in LGBTIQ+ and allies' artistic, political and activist engagement. Performing refusal carries *both* the potential of revolutionising art-forms, policies and social practices; *and* the potential of losing the engagement of other people which successful artistry, politics, business and activism rely on. Further, Queer strategies of refusal in artistry and activism can carry the risks of other retributions such as verbal or physical violence for individuals—and public heckling, media backlash and targeting. However they also carry the potential to be highly impactful. The individuals, groups and organisations explored here came to their refusal from different angles and motivations—nevertheless all had a valuable impact via social media during 2018.

References

Alcorn, G. (2016). 'She's just a happy little girl now': the Safe Schools effect on students. *The Guardian*. Retrieved from https://www.theguardian.com/australia-news/2016/dec/14/shes-just-a-happy-little-girl-now-the-safe-schools-effect-on-students

Arcand, R. (2018). Pussy Riot Release New Song Protesting Arrest of 18-Year-Old Girl. *Spin*. Retrieved from https://www.spin.com/2018/07/pussy-riot-unicorn-freedom-protesting-arrest-of-18-year-old-girl/

Australian Parliament Senate Legal and Constitutional Affairs Committee. (2018). *Legislative exemptions that allow faith-based educational institutions to discriminate against students, teachers and staff.* Canberra: Australian Parliament.

Belam, M. (2018). The LGBT athletes making history at the 2018 Winter Olympics. *The Guardian*.

Bredbeck, G. W. (2002). *Literary Theory: Gay, Lesbian, and Queer.* Chicago: New England Publishing Associates

Butler, J. (2004). *Undoing gender.* New York: Routledge.

Carpenter, M. (2018). The 'Normalization' of Intersex Bodies and 'Othering' of Intersex Identities in Australia. *Journal of Bioethical Inquiry, 15*(2), 1-9.

Copland, S., & Rasmussen, M. L. (2017). Safe Schools, Marriage Equality and LGBT Youth Suicide. In T. Jones (Ed.), *Bent Street.* Melbourne.

Correa, S. (2018). Gender Ideology: tracking its origins and meanings in current gender politics. *Sexuality Policy Watch, 2018*(5), 1.

Gadsby, H. (Writer) & J. Olb & M. Parry (Directors). (2018). Nanette [TV Special], *Netflix Comedy*. California: Netflix.

Griffiths, E. (2015). Same-sex marriage: Opposition Leader Bill Shorten introduces bill to Federal Parliament, urging MPs to 'step up'. *ABC News*. Retrieved from https://www.abc.net.au/news/2015-06-01/same-sex-marriage-bill-shorten-introduces-bill-parliament/6511208

Hawkins, S. (2016). *Queerness in Pop Music: Aesthetics, Gender Norms, and Temporality*. New York: Routledge.

Heller, A. (2005). *Immortal Comedy: The Comic Phenomenon in Art, Literature and Life*. Oxford: Lexington.

Hirst, J. (2018). Transgender children: doing it for the kids. *Archer*. Retrieved from http://archermagazine.com.au/2018/03/transgender-children/

Intersex Human Rights Australia. (2018). About Us. Retrieved from https://ihra.org.au/information/about/

Jagose, A. (1996). *Queer theory: An introduction.* New York: New York University Press.

Jones, T. (2013). How sex education research methodologies frame GLBTIQ students. *Sex Education: Sexuality, Society and Learning, 13*(6), 687-701.

Jones, T. (2016). Researching & Working for Transgender Youth: Contexts, Problems and Solutions. *Social Sciences, 5*(3).

Koziol, M. (2018). 'Heartbroken': Scott Morrison promises conscience vote on LGBTI students. *The Sydney Morning Herald.* Retrieved from https://www.smh.com.au/politics/federal/heartbroken-law-to-end-discrimination-against-lgbti-students-delayed-until-next-year-20181205-p50kal.html

Leah, R. (2018). Mike Pence offers blindingly disingenuous tweet to gay Olympian Adam Rippon. *Salon.* Retrieved from

Leibetseder, D. (2016). *Queer Tracks: Subversive Strategies in Rock and Pop Music.* London: Routledge.

Medhora, S. (2016). Safe Schools: Turnbull urges caution as Bill Shorten accuses him of giving in to 'the bullies'. *The Guardian.* Retrieved from https://www.theguardian.com/australia-news/2016/mar/17/safe-schools-turnbull-urges-caution-as-bill-shorten-accuses-him-of-giving-in-to-the-bullies

OII Australia. (2012). Briefing Paper on the proposed federal Human Rights and Anti-Discrimination Bill. Sydney: Organisation Intersex International Australia Limited.

OII Australia. (2013). Third Submission on the Involuntary or Coerced Sterilisation of People with Disabilities in Australia. Retrieved from http://oii.org.au/22613/third-submission-senate-inquiry-sterilisation/

Railton, D., & Watson, P. (2011). *Music Video and the Politics of Representation.* Edinburgh: Edinburgh University Press.

Reilly, K. (2018). Emma González Kept America in Stunned Silence to Show How Quickly 17 People Died at Parkland. *Time World.* Retrieved from http://time.com/5214322/emma-gonzalez-march-for-our-lives-speech/

Short, M. (2017). Penny Wong should be our next Prime Minister. *The Sydney Morning Herald.* Retrieved from https://www.smh.com.au/opinion/penny-wong-should-be-our-next-prime-minister-20171201-gzwu9o.html

Shorten, B. (2018). *Sex Discrimination Amendment (Removing Discrimination Against Students) Bill 2018 [No. 2]*. Canberra: Australian Parliament.

Tenplay. (2018). We Talk To New PM Scott Morrison About The Au Pairs, Political Bullying And 'Gender Whispering'. *The Project Season 10.* Retrieved from https://tenplay.com.au/channel-ten/the-project/extra/season-10/we-talk-to-new-pm-scott-morrison-about-the-au-pairs-political-bullying-and-gender-whispering

Twitter. (2018). Hateful Conduct Policy. *Twitter Rules and Policies.* Retrieved from https://help.twitter.com/en/rules-and-policies/hateful-conduct-policy

US House of Representatives Democrats Permanent Selection Committee on Intelligence. (2018). *Social Media Advertisements.* Washington: US House of Representatives Democrats Permanent Selection Committee on Intelligence Retrieved from https://democrats-intelligence.house.gov/facebook-ads/social-media-advertisements.htm.

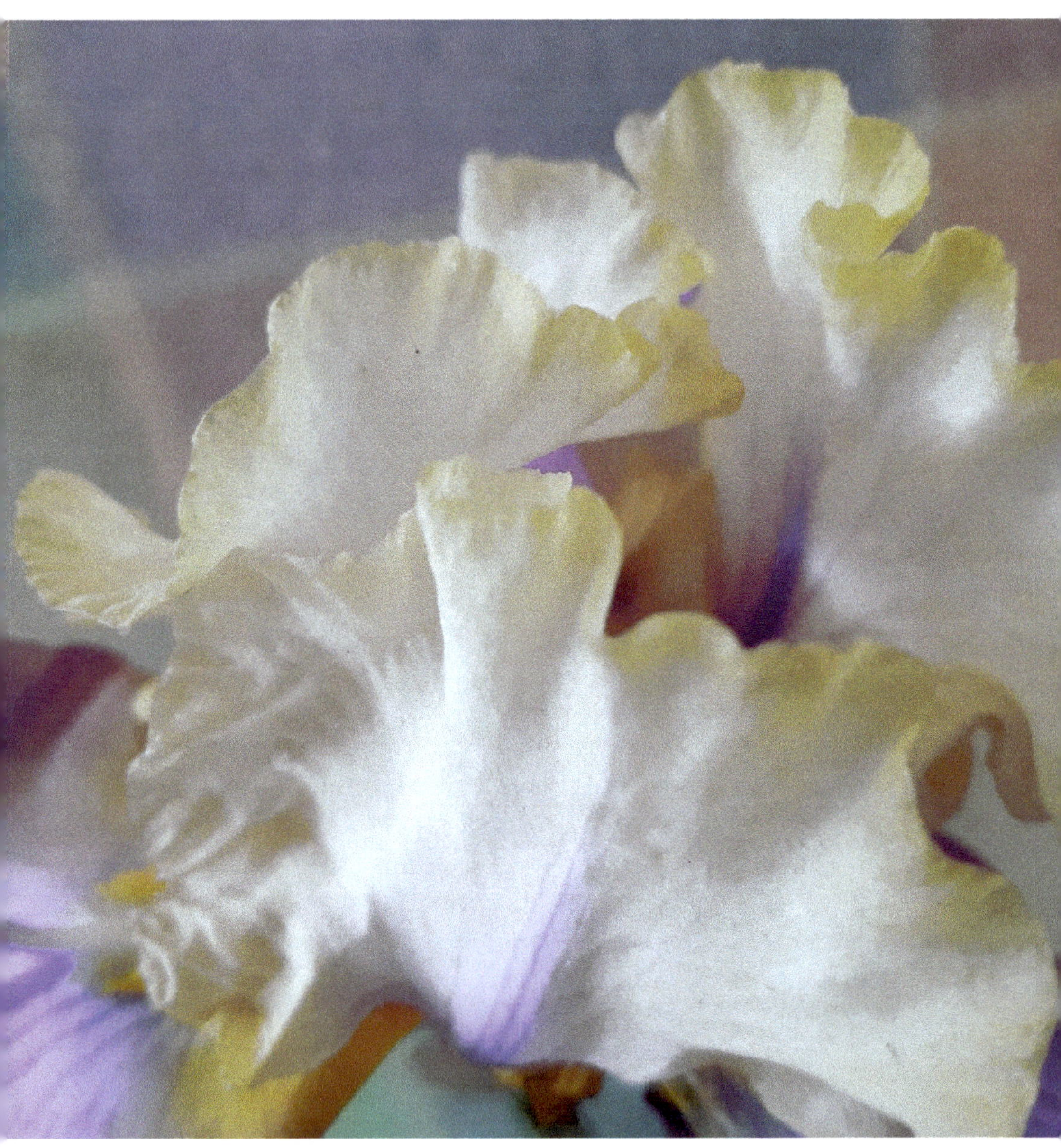

HENRY VON DOUSSA | IRIS 3

POETRY

Aurea Kochanowski

Tasseography

i. Over tea,
I tell him
I was queer all along.
And he says it is not true.
He tells me fairytales are not real.
    In a way, I understand –
I do not have the look about me.
The planets took no notice of my birth.
The ridge of my back is ordinary canvas,
and I do not summon rainclouds when I sing.
    But my queerness is undoubted –
when she kisses me,
my skin breaks out in stars.
I am a slow learner, but I still know the charm
for sewing myself a new face, a better name.
    Best of all, months of practice
have made my hands peculiar –
my favourite trick, when I reach
into long-empty pantries,
is to find one last bag of tea.

ii. Of my ilk, I am sometimes the youngest,
so I have not yet met a sphinx,
and all my spells resemble hairpins.
But there are common secrets with my kind –
we always notch the corners of our doors.
We are sure to keep

at least one wolf
asleep beneath the fireplace.
    There was a time
when strange blood was thought profane,
and many of us died.
So in springtime,
we gather in caves and hallways,
to remember them,
and remember us,
incredible us.
And we melt into each other.
We become strange lights in the night,
horned and glittering things
all smeared with many magics
so that we may not err in whom we love.

iii. In the morning,
once I have tidied the garden of crows,
I shall share the last teabag
with her, my kaleidoscope woman.
Of us all, she is best at tasseography.
She takes a cup
and reads the morning news to me,
while the kettle sings Aïda
and rainclouds roll across the ceiling.

René Bennett

Post-optimistic

Foreword

I thought I was prepared, was thoroughly, utterly ready for anything. The steps of the procedure, the physical pain, the recovery and limitations; all arranged into neat dot points inside my head, objectified, a means to an end. Hours spent online consuming success stories, 'after' photos and videos of shirtless people smiling down at their scars. I couldn't wait to be one of them, and for everything to change. On the brink of relief, there was no reason to consider anything beyond macro happiness, let alone brace for anything insidious. An oversight maybe, but who can really pre-empt how emotions will manifest in a transition? Especially those grounded in the very act of moving from pre to post, from anticipation to reality; in doing so relinquishing the kind of doe-eyed hope that one can only hold in the before. There was no real warning, no way to prepare for the birth of a new kind of dissonance. When I woke up after surgery, I was filled with gratitude. The sight of my chest was like applying ointment to a burn. Top dysphoria at long last was soothed, my identity and body finally intercepting. For the first time, I felt my true self become tangible, blatant, and to others, surely obvious. Yet the world continued to call me something which I am not, have never truly been. I was conflicted between my newly found inner peace and the contrary response from the external; felt cheated and left to ask questions that led into one another like a spiral: *How can they still fail to see? Will they ever see? What hope do I look toward now that my date has passed?* In the following months, I tried to assemble words into the form of a lens, into which I could look and derive clarity about these unanticipated feelings. This process of transforming mercurial emotion into written expression, like an itch on the brain. I had to scratch, had to create something out of the experience.

The result offered up below, still damp with the foggy residue of post-op depression …

*

Post-optimistic

I was used to people glancing and then making up their minds;
Auto-filing me as 'F' in the space behind their eyes.
These assumptions based on clay that was molded out of shape.
Mismatched pieces left to burn, embedding chaos into fate.
Such layered pain I sought to cleanse, by incisions made in flesh.
For who could get it wrong in the wake of absent breasts?
Intentions stretched out plain, by an eloquent public plea.
A letter shared, I'd told the world that I am not a '*she*'.
'*This will be hard to get used to*' was the generalised reply.
With sympathy I'd countered with '*I ask only that you try*'.
In some I found fierce allies, with '*they*' rolling off their tongues.
Saw others hit the like button and careless words continue on.
Still others closed their minds to my pursuit of affirmation;
Doubt-filled and dismissive of any heartfelt conversation.
My resolve withstood each challenge; despair quieted and quelled.
For my date was ever looming, a burden soon to be expelled.
Breathless, rushing forward; a giddy comet high in space.
The destination calling, with grand promises of change.
I was sure all would be different, after incisions made in flesh.
For who could still invalidate in the wake of absent breasts?
These thoughts swirled overhead as my wits began to fade.
Moments lost and then awake, vision foggy, dense and grey.
Compression vest and drains in tow, I had reached the other side.
Finally free to throw my shoulders back with nothing left to hide.
Unbridled grin at that first sight, shameless tears upon the floor.
The pure joy of seeing reflection begin to match with inner core.

Yet amidst euphoric throes, a dissonant pull within my brain.
For in spite of presentation, contrary language remained the same.
That hollow sound of familiar voices, still using terms assigned at birth.
Choosing to tend their own discomfort, revealing perceptions of my worth.
So naive were my expectations, of those incisions made in flesh.
It did not stop them inscribing '*she*' upon the flatness of my chest.
I had cut away the mismatch; an endeavour to feel whole.
Not one regret, yet bitter sweet; a lingering sadness in my soul.
Sustained no more by thoughts, of '***when*** *it's over, I'll be cleansed*'.
Left now to find new strength, to endure the other side of '*when*'.

Peter Mitchell

Three poems

Could I borrow the car?

I am a boy-on-a-mission. I climb the stairs to his office.
He's having lunch in Maitland Park. Forehead knotted.
I ride the motor to the park. Our family car noses the gutter.
My dad's in the driver's seat, another man in the passenger seat.
Infrared heat radiates the car. *I'll talk to you tonight.*
His hair is dishevelled. I ride away. The rippling air prickles my skin.

Chances

February 85. Another clinic visit. Same
old, same old
except
a tiny lump appears
in my left cheek.

After the consultation, I meet Ted
in Oxford Street.
How's your health? I ask.
Great!
The doctor's prescribed interferon and it's working.
There's a sixty per cent chance
of success.

It's early May.
The doctor smiles.
The tiny lump resolves.
You're today's healthy patient.

June.
Ted's obit
is in the
Sydney Star Observer.

Sight lines

1.
The ping-pong of first impressions starts it. The surfer desires
the flick of silken hair, the night-dark eyes; the composer
craves the sinew of shoulder, the muscle of an upper
arm. These illuminations alchemise into keepsakes.
After a year, their synergy morphs to love. For two more
years, they sleep in the ancient way: close, arms
and legs entwined; the rhythms of drowse
& dream, now shallow now vast.

2.
On their third anniversary, career carries the composer
to Boston. In seat 3A, winging through an ocean of sky,
his head rests, his eyes are closed. Behind them is the beach
where they met, his love's broad chest coming towards
him. Below him offshore from their meeting place, his lover
sits on a long board and his arms conduct the air. He looks
up, the plane now a hyphen, the ocean's swell his back-
ground. Eyes closed, recollections on the way-back
machine to that night, his lover's black-
haired swish like a conductor's flourish.

3.
These memories of love arouse the sky as infrared
ardor: resonant, heart garlands, nightly harvest.
But what language do they carry to the ear, the eye?
Music fades; water becomes savage; syllables are
shattered. These sight-lines of love are as insignificant as
a mosquito's death, a vivid life finished, on an open palm.

Tina Healy

We were the ones that went before

We were the ones that went before.
The ice breakers, the change makers,
Risk takers who stood against the flow,
To grow, to sew the change, to rearrange
the strange obsession with rigid roles,
That tore our souls at opposite poles
to the way we felt inside, no pride,
so we lied to ourselves, to live, to give
an illusion of love, and dull the war, the sore,
That hurt the ones that went before.

We were the ones who went before.
Ours was an uncouth truth, a stolen youth,
We lived a life you dictated, you stated,
we were slated for a cage, a rage, an ice age
where feeling is reeling from the sealing
of our hearts, our private part
that asks you for love as we are,
to heal the scar, the darkened star,
of grief, the thief of love's leaf
that washed upon the shore
of the ones who went before.

We were the ones who went before.
We stood before the doctor, the nurse,
the curse, of your perverse medical
hearse, that entombed and groomed,
We were doomed to jump the hurdles,
that girdled a sense of self that curdled

under your gawk at the way we walk and talk,
to get your approval, your privileged feudal
control of our bodies, that everybody
that was somebody in the psych profession
had discretion for suppression, the oppression
of the light that burns bright, our right to fight
for the gender that lays at the core
of the ones who went before.

We were the ones who went before.
We were the daughters that left your borders
over waters on society's orders
that our surgery a perjury, was a financial burglary
of the public purse, a curse, a raucous verse,
in a song that gonged something was wrong
in your ears, your fears,
when difference appears,
your hearts colded, your attitudes folded
they moulded as our planes flew home,
we arrived alone, nowhere for, no care for,
no one was there for
The ones who went before.

We were the ones who went before.
We jumped the hoops, the loops,
that conformity troops had put in place
to encase us, showcase us, like mice in a maze,
endless days, myriad ways to make us pay a price
to taste the spice, of the paradise
that beckoned we reckoned
when all was said and done.
So please don't forget the debt
the price that was set, for a generation
the formation, laid a foundation,
for a community that grew,
on the courage of a few,
we owe so much more,
To the ones who went before.

Madison Griffiths
Three poems

ON WOMEN

I.
HOW WILFULLY CRUEL ONE MUST BE
TO MARK DOWN 'NO' ONTO BALLOT PAPER—
AND YET STILL, BY WAY OF SEARCH BARS,
LOOK FOR 'YES' IN THE SHAPE OF
SEARCH?SEARCH=GIRL+ON+GIRL.

II.
TELL A WOMAN THAT HER SOFT, PULPY BRAIN IS NOT
HER GREATEST ASSET, AND SHE'LL LEARN TO TRUST
HER SOFT, PULPY BODY INSTEAD.
TELL HER THAT SHE IS ANIMAL INSTINCT, FLESH
AND SEX, AND SHE'LL SWALLOW YOU WHOLE WITH
HER FELINE INTUITION.
TELL A WOMAN THAT SHE IS NO MORE THAN
CARNAL FLAVOUR, AND SHE'LL EXPOSE YOU TO HER
LEONINE FLOCK.
SEE, WHEN WOMEN GATHER, MEN ARE (ALWAYS)
THE FIRST TO GO: USHERED OUT AND INTO THE SUN
BY SHE WHO SNARLS.

III.
AS TIME MARCHES ON, SO DO WOMEN.
SOME ON HARD GROUND, THEIR SLEEVES CUFFED
AND THEIR LACES TIED.

SOME ON THE SHOULDERS AND LAPS OF OTHER
WOMEN,
DEMANDING LIBERATION AS THEIR FOOTPRINTS
LEAVE BRUISES SHAPED LIKE INEQUALITY AND PITY
ON THE TIRED SKIN OF OTHERS:
OF THE WOMEN THEY FEAR AND TAUNT.
WHOSE BLOOD AND SWEAT IS WEDGED INTO THE
GROOVES OF YOUR SNEAKERS?

WITH WOMEN

I.

we kissed by a river
where a plastic fork on the greasy shore was our only witness
and later, in the honey light of your bedroom, you asked me about
my fears

HEIGHTS, i told you
like any new lover would

HEIGHTS, my darling
the ESCALATORS at parliament station
a NEEDLE, bleached and ready to embellish my naked arm
the sort of FOG that swallows up roads and sheep
distant
like tiny, white boulders
with tiny, white legs
unseeingly stumbling into some farmer's backyard BUTCHERY
or worse! SMOG
cloudy, human acid
(proof that we are failing)

II.

open WATER
where sea skeletons bear their stony teeth, hungry for toes
and the current
the way it curls and cries and guzzles, summoning plastic and flesh into its
ocean garden

we collapse into cotton sheets and
what I do not tell you is that in five years, it will be
YOU, my darling

i will see a pink body lathered in morning sweat by a lone traffic
light, yawning

and for a moment, i will mistake him for *YOU*
(don't look)
and he will mistake me for a contour of a woman, trembling in second-hand trousers
as you always did

in the purple cosmos of my sleep, you spit/kick/curse/strike/ at/in/on me
every day is a burial, my darling
deep seas
lamb that weep and march
your thumbs lodged into my shoulders, like meaty threats
heights, *my darling*
how much i have grown

III.

some people are easy to love—
'water once a fortnight' easy
easy to stick to walls, like blue tak
easy-like-sunday-morning easy
like zips and elastic
sleeping pills and dried flowers
easy like crosswords, and GPS directions
and takeaway cups, and one-size-fits-all 'easy'
and then there is you—
like ivy in the winter
and buttons
and stacks of spotted dishes
and shrunken wool
but you mustn't forget
that the plates and cutlery came from
dinner parties
and card games
and second-servings
and come spring, you'll climb every wall
and your leaves will thread their way
around every fence post—

every family of bricks
with such marvellous,
lovely,
undeniable
ease

NO

practice saying no.
rub it over your joints.
set it as your alarm.
hang it from the towel rack.
iron it onto fabric.
dog ear its pages.
tighten its straps.
tag it in the photographs.
store it under your pillow.
tuck it behind your ear.
pull it over your hips.
memorise how it tastes.

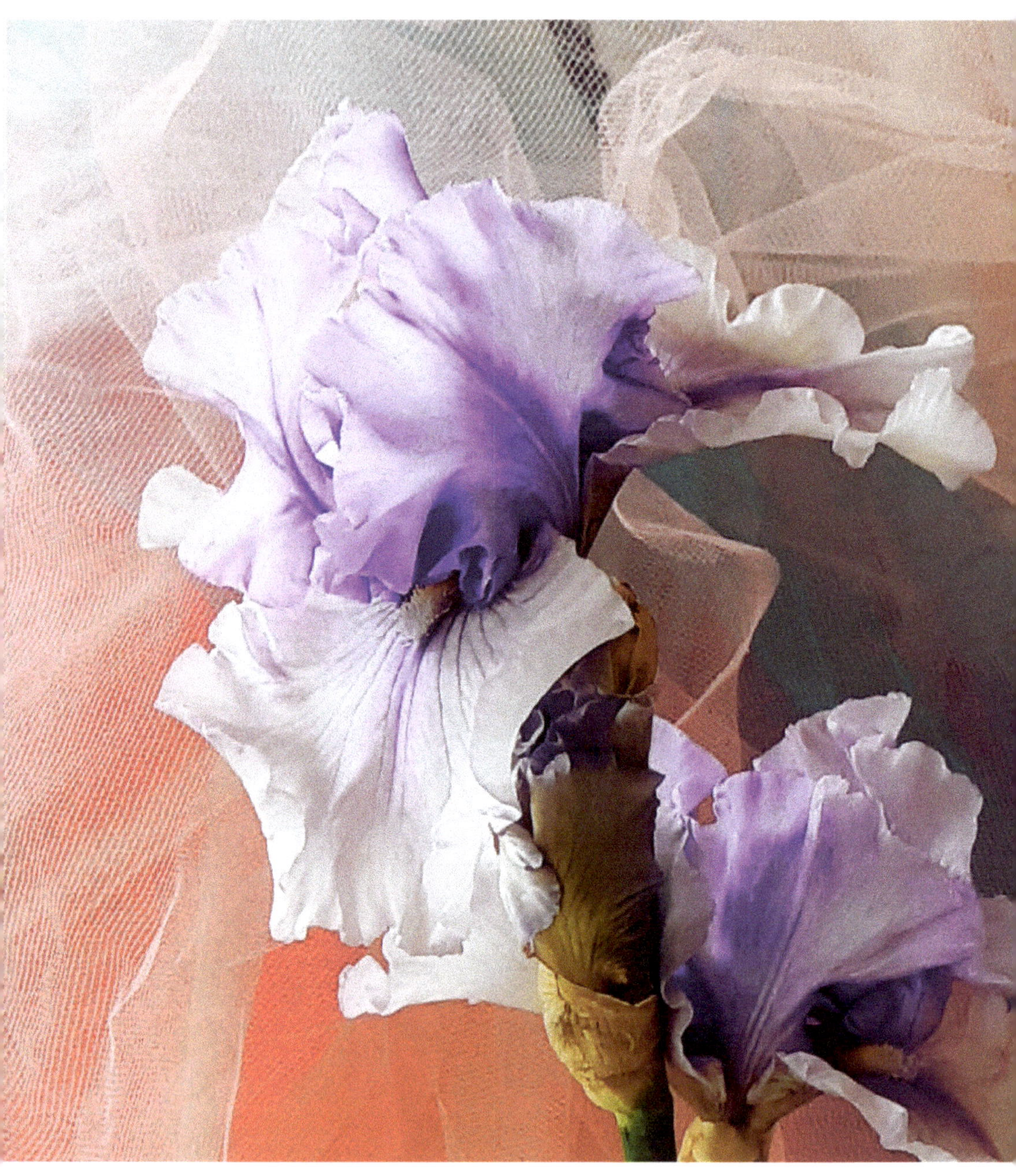

HENRY VON DOUSSA | IRIS 4

FICTION

Andy Murdoch
Island fragments

I

'It's the one thing we've always said about you,' my mother told me over the phone the afternoon before I flew to Greece by myself. 'You've always been happy with your own company.'

There was a period in primary school—maybe a few months, maybe closer to a year—where I had a lunchtime routine. I would eat the sandwiches my mother had packed for me that morning, sitting by myself behind the shelter sheds, and then I would go to the toilet, and then I would walk. From the toilet block I would walk past the basketball court to the northern end of the oval. I would walk around the oval and then, from the other end of the school, at the southern end of the oval, I would skirt the handball courts behind the oldest school building and walk between the newer buildings, past the speech therapy unit that had cured my lisp and the art building where the teacher would mock my efforts with what I guess she thought was affection. I would walk to the end of the school and then circle around the playground area until I found myself back at the toilet block.

And then I would do it again.

Eventually a teacher on yard duty realised what I was doing, day after day, week after week. 'What are you up to, mate?' he asked me one day.

'Just walking,' I said. 'Am I in trouble?'

'Of course not,' he said. 'Why aren't you playing with your friends?'

'I don't have any friends,' I said. It was really quite straightforward.

My teacher stared at me, horrified.

'That's true,' I told my mother. 'I am pretty happy with my own company. That's true.'

II

'I don't like the giant teddy bear, mummy,' the little boy says. He's drinking something. Hot chocolate, I guess.

'It's just a teddy, sweetheart.' She has a slight accent—not Middle Eastern, there's a twinge of posh London to it, her and the kid. Not strong though. 'It's just a big teddy, it's even got fur and everything!'

'It's creepy,' the little boy says. 'It's got some great big—*thing* hanging over its head. And I bet it's not real fur. I bet it's fake.'

The woman sighs. 'Even real teddy bears have fake fur these days, you know.'

If it's possible for a little boy—five? six?—to sneer, the little boy sneers. 'Don't be so silly, mummy.'

She doesn't pick up on this insolence. She drinks her coffee, and I drink mine, and the little boy licks the chocolate foam out of his paper cup.

'Darling, don't be disgusting.'

'It's yummy,' he says, a dark moustache of milky foam glistening on his upper lip. She doesn't pick up on that, either.

We're nowhere near the giant teddy bear sculpture that sits at the centre of the airport. We're at a cheap coffee place—not Starbucks, the other one—at the end of one of the airport's concourses. The coffee's not bad. I don't know where mummy and her little boy are going. I don't know if there's a daddy somewhere—somewhere in the airport, somewhere else. I don't know where they're going, but I'm flying to Greece, and I need to be at the other end of the airport soon.

I check the giant teddy's fur on the way through. I thought it was ceramic the first time I was here, but now I'm not sure.

III

I was sitting on my hotel balcony looking at the five identical balconies next to mine along the side of my hotel, and a voice behind me said, 'You can choose who comes out of the balcony doors. All five of them. But there are rules.'

'This is absurd,' I said. 'I'm just on holiday.'

'Rule number one,' the voice behind me said.

'Is there a reason you sound like Ian MacKellen?' A fair question, I thought.

'Rule number one,' the voice said. 'You cannot request the appearance of anyone you want to have sex with.'

I wanted to turn around and sneer at him, but I couldn't. 'That is the stupidest thing I've ever heard,' I said. 'What's the point of a fantasy game if that's rule number one?' Again, a fair question, I thought, but he didn't respond. 'So what's rule number two?'

He paused. 'Actually there isn't a rule number two,' the voice said. 'It's been a while since I've played this game. There's only rule number one, I forgot about that. So who comes out of the first balcony door?'

'You're not a very competent fantasy game host, are you, Sir Ian?' Sir Ian ignored this.

'A prince and a princess,' I said, because why the fuck not. 'Just after they've married.'

'You might want to have sex with the prince,' the voice said rather sternly.

'I don't do hetties,' I said. 'Or bi guys. Or closet cases. And if he's married …'

'That's really quite judgmental, you know,' the voice said. 'But … very well.' And just like that a prince and a princess stepped out onto the balcony next to mine, as pretty and well-dressed and bland as you'd expect. The prince was quite hot; if he'd been gay I'd have shagged him. 'Next,' said the voice.

'Mum and dad,' I said.

'Your father's dead.' Exasperation, was that?

'It's a fantasy game. How can death be a problem?'

A pause, and then a grudging 'Yes, yes,' and then there they were, just beyond the prince and princess. Northern Ireland vintage, I'd have said. Younger than I was on my balcony. That was a shock. Dad looked a bit confused.

'My ex,' I said, not waiting for the prompt.

'That's against …'

'—It's not,' and I nearly looked over my shoulder again. 'Trust me. It really isn't.'

And there he was. The day he'd told me. And I didn't. I really didn't.

'Two left,' the voice said.

'A fat man,' I said. 'A grossly, obscenely, morbidly obese fat man.'

'Obese and fat are tautological and there are those who find the larger frame sexually arousing.'

'Not me.'

Gandalf sighed. 'Dear me, you really are a most judgmental young man.'

'I'm not young.'

But there he was, on the balcony one down from my ex. He was very, very fat, the fat man.

'Last but not least,' the voice behind my shoulder said.

'A Greek Adonis,' I said. 'The most stunningly beautiful Adonis in all of the Greek islands.'

'But that's against …'

'—I won't be able to see him.' I smiled at my ex. It wasn't a pleasant smile, and he didn't smile back. 'He'll be behind the fat man, and the fat man's very fat, and I can barely see the fat man anyway behind the rest of them. And if I can't see him I can't want to have sex with him, can I?'

'Hmm,' rumbled the voice. 'There are those who'd disagree.'

'Oh fuck off, Gandalf,' I said.

'You could call him. What about *phone* sex? Sex chat lines?'

'Never done them,' I lied. 'I'm a very visual person.'

'Hmm.' But I knew I'd won.

'Oh, very well …'

And behind the fat man I saw what might have been the flicker of a balcony door open, the merest patch of what might have been golden skin. And then nothing.

'Well then,' the voice said. 'Satisfied?'

'No,' I said. 'Of course not. How could anybody be satisfied with that? What a stupid game. Are you? Are you satisfied?'

But there was no response.

IV

There was a cat on the island of Kimilos who was different to all the other cats. He looked like all the other cats—he was skinny and usually sick and he walked with a limp and one of his eyes had been scratched out in a fight with three other cats over a plate of leftover moussaka the cook from one of the beach restaurants had thrown out the back. He looked like all the other cats on Kimilos. But he was different.

He was a magical cat.

The cooks on Kimilos didn't usually throw out plates of moussaka. They didn't usually throw out lamb kleftiko, or rabbit stifado, or soukoukazia. They usually threw out the chips and egg stupid English tourists ordered for their dinner because they didn't like all that foreign stuff. They'd eat half a plate of chips and egg, the tourists, and leave the rest, because the island cooks didn't know how to cook bangers and mash, and the cooks of Kimilos would chuck the leftovers out the back—leftover cheese omelettes, and lambs fry with bacon—and the cats of Kimilos would eat the leftovers.

And when the magical cat ate these things he wasn't really eating them. It looked like he was eating them, like all the other cats, but the magical cat was really eating duck a l'orange, and steak tartare, and chicken cacciatore. These are strange things for a magical cat to eat on an island in Greece, because they're not very Greek, and not very good for a cat. But this was a magical cat, and this is what he ate.

And then one night the cook at the beach restaurant threw out half a plate of leftover chips and egg and found the magical cat dead. Earlier the cook had thrown out half a plate of leftover moussaka, and the magical cat had fought over it again, and this time he lost more than an eye.

The cook didn't know the dead cat was a magical cat, but he was. He had been. It's the moussaka that gets them, every time.

V

At the top of the hill there was a rock, and on top of the rock sat a goblin. 'You have three choices,' the goblin said.

'For fuck's sake,' I said. 'I think I've been here already.'

'Not here,' said the goblin. 'Not here geographically, and not here metaphysically, either. Gandalf was different.'

'Jesus, even the fucking goblins call him Gandalf.' I'd quite enjoyed the hike to the top of the hill. There'd been a cave with a sacred fresco and some disintegrating statuary and a lovely view across the sea to Turkey. I wasn't enjoying the goblin.

The goblin blinked. 'His name's Gandalf,' the goblin said. 'And I'm not a goblin. I'm a frog. I'm a frog that's been turned into a goblin. By a wicked wizard. That's where your choices come in.'

It was my turn to blink. 'This is fucking insane,' I said. 'What the fuck is a frog that's been turned into a goblin by a wicked fucking wizard doing sitting on top of a rock on top of a hill on a Greek fucking island?'

The goblin blinked again. 'You swear a lot, don't you?'

'Yes,' I said. 'I swear a lot. I swear a fucking shitload.' My ex had said that about me, too. The goblin looked a bit like my ex, I thought unkindly. 'So what are my choices?'

Unkind, and untrue.

'Right,' said the goblin. 'So you can choose to turn me back into a frog. Or you can choose to leave me as I am. Or …' The goblin blinked again. And cleared its throat.

I waited. 'Or?'

'Or,' said the goblin, and cleared its throat again, 'or, you can choose to turn me into a prince.'

Again, my turn to blink. 'A prince.'

'A prince.' The goblin shrugged. 'Call it poetic justice.'

'And what if I choose not to choose?' I was pretty sure I had him there. 'What if I choose to just turn around and walk back down the hill?'

'Well, fairly obviously,' the goblin said, 'that would be choosing to leave me as I am.'

'Ah. Yes. Okay.' I thought about that for a few seconds. 'What if I choose to turn you into a prince and I find the prince sexually attractive? Despite knowing that the prince had previously been a goblin that had previously been a frog?' It wouldn't have turned me off, to be honest. 'What happens then?'

'That's against the rules,' said a voice behind my shoulder.

VI

'Slightly peculiar, heartbroken, criminally unpublished middle-aged writer lives out his years alone in a windmill on a hillside,' my friend said. 'There's a book in that, don't you think?'

'Do you think I'm slightly peculiar?' I looked at her. 'I don't think I'm remotely peculiar. Most of my friends back home think I'm the blandest person they know.'

'Your boyfriend of sixteen years dumps you and three weeks later you're on a remote Greek island thinking about buying a windmill to live in,' my friend said. 'That seems slightly peculiar to me.'

She wasn't really my friend. She was an English tourist staying at my hotel, and on my first night we'd had a drink and started talking. I did more of the talking than she did.

'It's a bit of a dump,' I said, to change the subject.

We were standing outside a windmill on a hillside on a Greek island. It was for sale. I'd found it on a Greek real-estate website.

'I think it's kind of cool,' she said. 'The pictures are, anyway. It's a bit more … dilapidated than I expected.'

'It doesn't have a roof,' I said.

I don't know why I'd searched Greek real-estate websites. When I found the windmill I'd shown it to her, and the website had a map, and it had been her idea to hike up the hill and find it. There was a for-sale sign out the front. I assume it was a for-sale sign. It was in Greek.

'It's got a roof,' she said. 'There are just a few holes in it. I'm sure there's some strapping young tradesman in town who'd fix that for you in a jiffy.'

I wasn't really thinking about buying a windmill on a Greek island. I don't think I was.

I walked across to the windmill and tried to look in through the window, but I couldn't see a thing.

VII

He looked at the watch. He looked at the sea.

The ferry chugged its way towards Piraeus. He had a cabin for the night, and it was already dark. He was standing at the back of the ferry. The sea was black, the churn phosphorescent.

He looked at the watch.

He'd been given the watch, a gift from his boyfriend their first Christmas together.

No. Ex-boyfriend. That's why he was in Greece.

There was an engraving on the back of the watch. 'Mister Magoo, 2002'. That's what his ex-boyfriend called him, because he was bald, and his eyesight was awful. Mister Magoo.

No. His ex-boyfriend didn't call him that. His boyfriend called him that. His ex-boyfriend didn't call him anything.

He looked at the sea. So much water, so far from home. He smiled. He'd tried to write while he'd been away. He'd failed. He'd failed. You're not running away, his friends had told him before he flew out. You're giving yourself space. But he had run away. And he'd achieved nothing. He'd spent two months on the islands, expecting to write, expecting a text, an email. I've fucked up. Please come home.

No text. No email.

No writing.

Sixteen years, and then: someone else.

He looked at the engraving. He turned the watch over.

He looked at the sea.

He was contemplating a *Titanic* moment. Camp, he knew. Open his hand, turn it, let the watch fall into the water. The blackness. The churn. The phosphorescence. Go back to his cabin, open a bottle of wine, drink the lot, go to sleep, wake up, get off the ferry at Piraeus, catch the metro to Athens airport, fly home.

Watch at the bottom of the sea.

He stood at the back of a Greek ferry on its way back to Piraeus.

He looked at the watch. He looked at the sea.

Holly Zwalf

Conga line

'The only good thing about a cruise is getting off,' my hairdresser had quipped with a smirk earlier that week, handing me a roll of condoms along with my change. 'Have one for me, honey, but when your knees are wrapped round your ears and you're banging so hard on that porthole that the ship's threatening to do a Titanic on our last remaining iceberg, don't forget that it was me who got you where you are by giving you good hair.' As he waved me out the door my phone vibrated against my hip.

'Brewton,' Aunt Aggie barked out before I'd even had a chance to say hi. 'Remember to pack some socks. The aircon on the Himalayan Isles trip was fucking cold. And bring your own toilet paper. They use two ply but three is so much more luxurious.' She dragged out the urrrrr in luxurious as though she were savouring the very thickness of the paper on her tongue. 'You need a costume for the last night. 'Seamen and Sirens'. Sirens as in mermaids, not police sirens.'

'And seamen as in …?'

'What?'

'Nothing.'

'Pay attention, Brewton. Don't forget some ozone blocker glasses and a hat for when you're out on deck. The ones with the neck flaps are best. And be at Katoomba ferry terminal at 10am sharp. I don't want to miss out on getting reservations for the Gilmore Girls Retrospective on ice. So please. Be. On. Time.' She rang off abruptly.

I was almost coming to regret offering to keep the old bitch company for the week. To be honest, being stuck on a boat for six days with a bunch of pensioners and overeaters was my idea of hell, but I'd agreed to chaperone my aunt because she liked to have company at dinner, and because she was old, childless, and Landed—she owned her own house. As the sea levels had risen so had the property prices, and we'd now hit a point where 80% of the population were living in the Leura slums, shipping containers stacked on shipping containers stacked on shipping containers. It was hard to remember a time when a shipping container had been considered a hip place to live. Agatha rented out her house for a phenomenal amount of money—enough to keep her permanently in cruises. Apparently in the old days a cruise had been cheaper than a nursing home. The only people who could afford one these days were still the pensioners, but now it was because they were the only ones who were Landed. Them and the Packer-Murdochs.

*

Ever since the Big Melt had started eating away at viable landmass, cruises had become the new black, the new Bali, the new New York. In fact there was even a New York cruise you could do where you could putter past the Statue of Liberty's crown, round the tip of the Empire State Building, and have lunch on Rockefeller Island. All sightseeing had to be done from inside, though, ever since some American refugees had pulled a poor couple off the deck when the ship had got too close to the shore, and tried to surreptitiously trade places. Apparently it had been their accents that had given them away, asking where the bathroom was instead of asking for the toilet. No one who's Landed says 'bathroom' these days.

*

The teeth were blinding. From the start of the gangway all the way to our berths, our path was flanked by wildly grinning crew—everyone from the captain to the cleaner was there to flash their expensively bleached smiles. My Aunt had booked us adjoining rooms—in case she got stuck on the toilet in the middle of the night was my assumption. I dropped my day bag on my bed, untucked the blanket and sheets (I can't stand a tightly-made bed), shoved the cardboard sign declaring 'Welcome Brewton! Remember: fun for all, all for fun!' in the bin, and then went back out into the hallway to wait for Aunt Aggie. As I was closing my door an overweight old queen puffed past me, dragging a suitcase behind him.

'I never trust the staff with my junk,' he lisped in that affected gay accent I hate, by way of explanation for his suitcase, and then gave me a once-over and a knowing grin. 'Looks like we're going to be cabin boys together.' He winked, as he stuck a key in the door next to mine.

Thankfully Aunt Aggie appeared at that point. She was eager to get straight to the bridge table, so once I had seen her to her chair and propped her up safely with a garish welcome cocktail in hand, I set off to find the nearest bar. If I was going to get through the week alive I'd be needing plenty of booze. After a detour past the badminton courts, two pools, and several forests of potted palms, I found my way to the Blue Lagoon, a sunken indoors bar on the seventh deck with aqua coloured lighting and an 80s cover band. I didn't want to have to tackle the crowds again too quickly so I ordered two beers and then swam through the smokey air to a table in the corner, as far from the band as possible. I'd just settled into my second drink when the band struck up a remake of the Vengaboys remake 'We're Going To Ibiza', except they'd changed the words to 'oh, we're going to Tuvalu' in an attempt to ironically reference the first of the land masses to have gone under in the Big Melt. Suddenly a fleshy hand had grabbed mine and I was tugged from my chair and pulled into a writhing conga line. The woman clamped my hands around her waist and wiggled off, her tight pink bike pants and purple bum bag wobbling in my face. I was about to escape when I felt another pair of hands snake around my waist, holding me firmly in place in the line. I glanced back to see a hungry looking woman with identical bike pants and bum bag grinning at me. She had a miniature frothy veil pinned to her ponytail, and the words 'Hen's Angels' printed across her breasts. I was a gay man trapped in the middle of hetero hell. We wove around the tables picking up more people as we went, until the entire bar was joined together groin to arse groin to arse, snaking around the room. As the song ended the band's frontman chuckled into the microphone.

'Well done folks, and welcome to Sailaway Cruises! Now every time you hear the opening bars of that song this week, the rule is that anyone within earshot has to join the conga line. Fun for all, and…' He held the microphone out to the crowd, as though we were at the Big Day Out or something.

'… all for fun!' the crowd screamed back.

'And if you refuse, what'll you have to do?'

'Walk the plank! Walk the plank!', the regular cruisers in the crowd yelled joyously, pumping their fists in the air.

*

Rumour had it there was a gay meetup called the Kylie Klub, every evening at sunset on the fourth deck. I told Aunt Aggie I had had too much sun that afternoon and was going to have a lie down. She barely looked up from her cards. I changed into my tightest tank top and a tiny pair of shorts, and ran some product through my hair. I'd made a pact with my personal trainer to only take the stairs, so I circumnavigated the lift queue and begrudgingly left the aircon to scale the first flight.

'Honey,' he'd warned me, 'you can gorge yourself at the buffet, but never ever do I want to hear about you taking the lift between decks.'

Why do gay men always call each other honey, I wondered idly, as I sweated it out climbing the stairs. Three flights later I emerged onto a nearly deserted sunlounge area, complete with real sand and dotted here and there with beach balls, buckets and spades, and other nostalgic beach paraphernalia. The moment I spotted the Kylie Klub I realised there was no point getting any closer. It was just a bunch of sad old queens, my neighbour included, drinking Gone Island Iced Teas in aquamarine resort wear and ozone-blocker visors. If I was going to get laid on this journey, clearly I was going to have to screw one of the crew.

Dinner that night was a sombre affair. Aunt Aggie had lost a friend at bridge, and he was now down in the ship's morgue, chilling.

'This is the problem with getting old, Brewton,' she sniffed into her prawn cocktail.

'Everyone starts fucking dying on you. You can't play bridge with three players, you know.'

I patted her hand gently and passed her another dinner roll.

'I think I'll pass. I'm going to call it a night.'

I walked her to her room. 'Do you need any help getting into bed?' I asked.

'Bugger off, Brewton. Go enjoy your youth while you've still got it.' She patted me on the cheek and closed her door.

I was at a bit of a loss of what to do. I had already had my fill of the trashy bars, and I hadn't bothered making any reservations for the onboard shows. I wandered about aimlessly for a while but got caught up in another conga line near the ice sculptures, so once that had ended I went below decks and sought refuge in the casino. At least there everyone was too zombified by their little flashing machines to take time out to do the conga. The brittle air tinkled with pokie jingles, undershot with the occasional baritone hoot when a roulette wheel turned up the goods. I spent some time making eyes at a cute croupier before security started to get edgy, and then I took myself off to bed for a wank.

*

I was sitting poolside the next day in my water-proof ozone suit when a siren started up, and everyone in the pool swiftly got out.

'Brown alert, brown alert,' some kids screeched as they raced out of the pool.

'What's a brown alert?' I asked the woman lounging next to me.

She looked at me with raised eyebrows, but when she realised I was serious informed me that it meant someone had done a shit in the pool. It must have been several giant shits, because by the afternoon the pool had been drained and a sign erected explaining that it would remain empty for several days, until the desalination plant could generate enough water for a refill. The other two pools swelled with annoying families as a result, and the splashing screaming kids were more than I could handle, so I took to reading and napping in my room between meals. It was amazing how quickly I had converted to cruiseship life. It was all about the food. In the mornings we ate at the Sunny Side Up cafe, which had real poached eggs from the ship's chickens, and an incredibly convincing synthetic smashed avocado on toast. Lunch was a two hour affair at one of the five onboard buffets, allowing for a conga line or two round the tables, and most nights Aunt Aggie and I ate at the Captain's table. It was supposedly the most sought-after table on the ship, reserved for the people in the suites and long-termers like Aggie, but I never actually saw the fabled Captain. The class structure on board was positively retro, as was the way all the menial staff were brown skinned, while the people in charge were all white. The whole ship was like a floating colonial time warp. The free buffets were an all you can eat affair teeming with lobsters and crabs and prawns. Delicacies like beef and chicken and pork, however, were only available in Seagrass, a restaurant on level ten which you paid for separately. Having come from the Leura slums, where most meals came in a glass in the form of a protein shake, it almost made me feel nauseous watching perfectly good apples, loaves of bread, and cheeses all get swept into the bins at the end of each meal. However the nausea might have also been attributed to the unusually rough seas. I'd heard murmurings that the currents were behaving strangely, and that the Big Melt was somehow to blame.

*

Every night after dinner Aunt Aggie insisted that I chaperone her to the lounge bar for Croaky Karaoke. The rules were that you could only compete if you were over 75, but that seemed to be the mean age of at least half the people on the boat so there was a long list of competitors to get through. Everyone was desperate to win because the prize was to sing a duet on the final night with an old crooner called Justin Bieber. All the old bats were batty over him, Aunt Aggie no exception.

'I know what you're up to, Brewton,' she hissed, when on the third night I complained. 'You've got your eye on my house; I've got my eye on Justin Bieber. I need your vote, so suck it up.'

Every night we sat there for hours, waiting for her name to be called, applauding the geriatric wannabe Madonnas and Beyonces and Lady Gagas (but not too loudly because votes were partly based on the amount of decibels registered when the audience cheered at the end of your song). I was fairly certain my cheersquad abilities were the real reason Aggie had invited me on the trip.

'Seamen and Sirens' night came round faster than I'd expected. It was a relief to realise our time onboard was nearly at an end, though to be honest I'd started to be lulled by the conveyor belt rhythm of being fed, watered, and entertained on repeat. I decided to brave a bar for my final night onboard, and seeing as Aunt Aggie had given up on her karaoke dreams the night before when her rendition of *Frozen's* 'Let It Go' had failed to raise the roof, I was free to go as I pleased. The best action seemed to be happening back at the Blue Lagoon. There were the usual Little Mermaid red wigs and tails, a group of hot guys in full navy regalia, a few King Trident staffs and fake beards, and some smart bugger who had just tied a plastic bag on his head and was telling anyone who'd listen that he was a used condom. Most people just wore a sailor's cap with their normal clothes, though, because most people hadn't read the 'before you board' email, and the caps were only five bucks in the Ship Shop. Problem was, it made it hard to tell the civvies from the crew, which is why the announcement didn't get taken seriously until the next morning. Someone stood on a chair and started yelling about Katoomba going under and a war between the Himalayas and the Alps, but it got swallowed up in a raucous call for 'conga!!!' as the band struck up their theme song. I'd been keeping my eye on a tasty young thing working behind the bar, and was drinking fast and tipping high, trying to lure him over. Unfortunately I soon had company—my neighbour, all dragged up as Ursula the sea witch with blue lipstick sliding down his face, and tentacles sewn on to his shirt. We were apparently in competition, but I reassured myself that even if he was tipping higher, I was the one with youth and looks on my side.

*

I woke up in the morning with a tentacle poking into my butt cheek. It took me a while to realise the tentacle was actually another kind of appendage. Worse still it appeared it was attached not to the slick young barman, but to Ursula. Oh sweet jesus what had I done? I eased myself out from under the snoring bulk and shrugged on my clothes as quietly as possible, trying to recall how it had all gone so wrong, but my head was too fuzzy to remember. I consoled myself with the thought that at least we were docking today. I'd never have to see him again. I had the hangover from hell, and my head was thumping hard. No, actually, that wasn't inside my head, I slowly realised. I could hear thumping from the decks above, and the soft roar of voices. Confused, I slipped out the door, to find the corridor full of frantic passengers. I spotted Aunt Aggie holding a cocktail glass and slumped against the wall, and rushed over.

'It's all gone,' she moaned.

'What's all gone?' I asked, panic rising slowly in my throat.

'There's no ice left.'

'At the bar?'

'No you stupid fuck, in the poles. The last sheet has melted. My house has gone under.

Everyone's at war with everyone and there's no safe port to land. We're stuck on this fucking boat for ever.'

*

Up on deck some people were hurling themselves over the railings, while others were surging towards the bars. I joined the scrum, desperate for some hair of the dog. The bar staff were nowhere to be seen, so everyone was just helping themselves, the smart ones stashing bottles down trousers for future safekeeping. The band, however, were all in their places, singing 'We All Live In A Yellow Submarine' and crying drunkenly in between verses. A crackle erupted from the loudspeakers hidden in the palms, and then a voice filled the bar.

'This is your captain speaking.'

The band stopped playing and a hush fell over the crowd. I was relieved to discover there was a captain after all.

'From now on the buffet will not be all you can eat.'

There was a murmur of discontent from the crowd.

'At our most recent calculation this ship has enough food in the buffet to last us another three days, but only on tight rations. We are also in the process of excavating the waste disposal units to salvage what we can.'

Another murmur from the crowd, this time accompanied by the sound of people retching.

'However we have good news. Sailaway Cruises have been preparing for the end of the Big Melt for some time, and our passengers will be pleased to hear that the tropical garden on level two is currently producing all the fruit and vegetables consumed on this ship. Thanks to the fishing club we have a steady supply of seafood, and the desalination plant is providing us with drinking water as we speak. If we exercise extreme caution we are confident that the cruise can go on …'

'… and on, and on …' interrupted the lead singer of the band, doing a convincing impression of Celine Dion's smash hit.

'… indefinitely.'

Cheers erupted from the crowd, and someone popped a party popper.

'However in the interest of keeping up morale, anyone found not adhering to the spirit of this ship will be forcibly removed. It is important that we work together in times like these. This ship's motto is 'fun for all, all for fun,' and we will be enforcing this where necessary.'

As everyone hooted and hugged each other, I noticed out of the corner of my eye several crew members appear, taking up posts at each exit. The band struck up the opening bars of 'Oh, we're going to Tuvalu' and I started for the door, but it was barred by a brawny crew member with arms folded. He stared me down stonily.

'Everyone must conga, or walk the plank', he said, and nudged me back onto the floor, where I got swept up by a joyful Ursula who grabbed me by the hips and propelled me groin to arse into the midst of the conga line.

The band played on and on.

Lian Low
Hyperreality

Hyperreality is a monologue I wrote in the mid-1990s, when I was just coming to terms with my lesbian sexual identity. At the time, the only training I had in playwriting was a devout attention to diarising my day-to-day experiences, which I began when I was 14 and continued all the way to the end of high school. Through various interpersonal interactions at school and university, I was constantly reminded of my foreignness, my heavy accent, my un-Australian migrant body. On top of that I bottled-up my intense crushes on women. And I was painfully, painfully shy.

At the end of high school, I saw an advertisement for the Irene Mitchell Inaugural Short Play Competition in *The Age*. I'm not sure what compelled me to submit. I had no role models in my family who loved literature as much as I do. However, I'd just completed high school co-aceing the 'advanced English' Literature class with another classmate. I had a knack for language, and so I submitted because I felt like I had a good story to tell. I didn't think twice that in 1996, on a predominantly white theatrical stage, judges may not be so kind to a Chinese-Malaysian Melbourne-based migrant lesbian coming out and being infatuated with kd lang.

There were 100 entries in the competition, judged by *The Age* senior critic, Helen Thomson, and journalists John Mangan and Pamela Bone. I won the Under-25 category, was awarded $1,000 and a rehearsed playreading at the George Fairfax Studio, Victorian Arts Centre. When it came to casting, the producers had to fly a WAAPA (Western Australian Academy of Performing Arts) based graduate actor, Fiona Choi, to perform. There wasn't an Asian Australian actor in Melbourne they could find to play an 18-year-old Chinese-Malaysian-Australian woman. Two decades later, Fiona Choi now plays Benjamin Law's infamous mother in the acclaimed television series, *The Family Law.* She's now surrounded by talented Asian-Australian actors from a range of ages and genders. But, since writing the play, what hasn't changed much is homophobic and transphobic social mores. While anti-discrimination laws exist, social attitudes haven't really shifted. In 2014, a report *Growing up Queer*, on issues facing young Australians who are sexually diverse and gender variant found:

> Almost two-thirds of the 1032 young people who completed the survey experienced some form of homophobia and/or transphobia, with some experiencing multiple forms of abuse—64% had been verbally abused, 18% physically abused, and 32% experienced other types of homophobia and transphobia. Schools were identified as the major site in which homophobia and transphobia prevailed. Peers were most frequently the source of this homophobia and transphobia, but for many, it was the homophobia and transphobia perpetrated by some teachers that had the most profound impact in their lives.

I feel lucky that my favourite teacher in high school, my literature teacher, who I'd showed my finished draft to, didn't humiliate me about the content of my play. My gratitude for this crucial turning point in my life still remains. While there was no talk about sex and sexuality within my family context, writing about it was a way of making sense of the largesse, wonder, pain and beauty of the world of sex, sexuality, passion and love. And being true to myself.

HYPERREALITY DRAFT 3.0

Cast: GIRL/WOMAN or G/W—A young Chinese woman, 20s.
VOICE/ MONSTROUS-GHOST-LIKE FIGURE—
GIRL/WOMAN's mother, 50s.

Setting: The GIRL/WOMAN's bedroom; her sanctuary. *kd lang, Tracy Chapman and Buddha posters cover* ***GIRL/WOMAN****'s four bedroom walls.*

Time: Mid 90s. kd lang, Melissa Etheridge and Tracy Chapman have just burst onto the mainstream music scene to critical acclaim. There is also a new flourishing of queer representation - films like *Incredibly True Adventures of Two Girls in Love* and *Go Fish* have mainstream releases. *Lunch time.*

GIRL/WOMAN has just had a very stiff Saturday lunch with her mother. Mother asks her to clean the room. G/W storms into her room, yells, 'Leave me alone-lah, Ok or not , Maaa?' Agitated, she walks into her room, flustered. She's struggling with living with her mother, but she's too scared to leave. She picks up the remaining kd lang posters on the table and sticks them on the wall. She looks in the mirror, annoyed with her pimply face. When she finishes sticking up the posters, she walks around agitated for something to do.

GIRL/ WOMAN: Do you want to know how … *bored* … whatever … I feel? I'll tell you.

I'm waiting, just waiting, waiting to bleed.

Sounds stupid right? Who waits to bleed?

My boobs and tummy are so swollen, and my face is all pimply, I just wish it would come!

Imagine the inconvenience of waking up and then finding your groin and undies in a red pool. Like I'm a murderer. Of my own body. I hate my period. I really, really hate it. I wish I didn't have periods.

(Talks like an advocate)

Boys don't have periods
Boys can piss standing up
Boys talk and people listen
Boys can get drunk & go topless and no one cares.
Boys can hold hands with girls in public
Boys can kiss girls in public.
But I can't. I'm not supposed to, because *I'm a girl.*

G/W puts on kd lang's 'Constant craving' and rocks herself.

Actually, I'm just waiting, waiting for love to happen. Fall into my arms one day, like a miracle. Like *kd lang*. I've videoed her whenever she's on TV, cut-out articles about her from random magazines.

(Reminisces) Ingenue her first big hit album, was my first album. I have *Ingenue* on cassette and CD! I also have *Salmonberries*, her first film. And I have all her country and western albums!

When she was on *Hey, Hey It's Saturday*, I sent the producers a drawing I did of her, but I didn't get a response.

(*Addressing audience … support*) Oh, dear Lord Buddha, my darling baby brother ***tapes videos*** of kd for me.

(*Addressing herself … struggle*) Doesn't he know that she's, you know, one of those? I don't like saying lesbian. To me, it sounds wrong, dirty, perverted.

(*Addressing audience … support*) But dear, dear, dear Lord Buddha, you know a month or so back I was watching the Pride March, and there I saw my darling baby brother in the crowd as well. Then, at the Melbourne Queer Film Festival he was in the audience. He is one of the most supportive brothers in the world. I can't believe how supportive my baby brother is, that I would just keep bumping into him at all these queer events I'm at.

G/W hunches over on the bed.

Today is boring. The waiting. The nothing. (*checks undies*) Like my boring love life.

G/W falls onto bed star-shaped.

(Conversationally) But two weeks ago, it was the most exciting day of my life. (*bubbling with excitement*)

My uncle, Roger, had invited me to the NGV cos there was an exhibition of gamelan instruments, and he knows I'm interested in this. I arrive a bit early, and wait by the waterwall. My uncle arrives. With him, his housemate. This housemate of his is everywhere with him—at all the family birthdays, Christmases, Chinese New Years. The only thing they don't do together is go to the same church. I don't really like my uncle's housemate Dickie.

He's always very awkward around me, a bit cold. He doesn't really talk much. Actually, my uncle doesn't really talk much either and is awkward, and can be a bit cold. They both have the same personalities.

Anyway, hanging out with them is NOT the most exciting thing that happened to me. *Please!* We were in front of a Picasso, when just beyond a wall cavity, I spied ***kd*** with her ***girlfriend.***

I stifled a scream and smiled goofily at Roger and Dickie.

'What is it?' my uncle asks.

I just smiled. I couldn't speak. Then Dickie says, 'Oh my god, Roger, it's kd lang.'

The three of us huddled to the wall cavity.

G/W appears to hug her uncles

I wanted to run and touch kd, but I couldn't. I wanted to hold kd's hand. I wanted to be her girlfriend.

A loud voice interrupts the GIRL/WOMAN's engrossed self-chatter ...

VOICE *(off-stage):* Oiiiiiii! Come and help wash the dishes!!

Extract from 'Hyperreality' by Lian Low, in *Living and Loving in Diversity* (2018), Wakefield Press. *Living and Loving in Diversity* was launched at the 2018 AGMC National Conference, 'Living, Loving, Inspire', in Melbourne in September.

James May
Two wild outlaws

Sometimes I saw her shoot across a road before anyone could pin her down. Sometimes she was kicking back at a club on Oxford Street. She carved her way through that place—the tattoo of a serpent marked her stride. She lived in a rambling house in Surry Hills and danced at peep shows in Kings Cross. Now and then I saw her strutting through Taylor Square, missing a stiletto, puffing smoke in the air. Her spirit was bruised but she carried herself with dignity. She fought for friends who lost their way no matter how often they let themselves down. She hung in there because she knew what it was like to be queer in a straight world. She knew what it was like to be afraid. She knew how it felt to be judged. Her name was Aunt Ruby.

*

We hopped on our bikes and pedalled through Darlinghurst, rolling up at terraces in crumbling alleys. She rapped on doors, picking stuff up, dropping things off. Money changed hands and we took off, flying down Crown Street—two wild outlaws. William Street was flooded with cars streaming into The Cross. We jumped off our bikes and cruised the footpath, the neon red Coke sign bold and bright. Hookers paraded outside the laundry on Bourke—skin-tight blouses on waif physiques, leather minis hitched up long slender legs. Cars pulled over and they swaggered to the kerb puffing cigarettes.

Ruby and I hit Darlinghurst Road—it was like dipping our toes in a snake-pit. A cacophony of techno music, tinkering poker machines, footsteps smacking concrete. I followed Ruby into shops, cafes, dirty book stores. She was always quick, light on her feet. We slipped past blokes in caps, faces buried in smutty magazines. She got chummy with queens in slick coats, stuffing pills in pockets and texting phone numbers. Junkies scurried in and out like rats. They hit up smack in grubby cubicles and slunk out with forlorn eyes.

The night rolled on and we hit the clubs—a world of neon sleaze. The sound of Iggy Pop raged inside … '*Sweet sixteen in leather boots.*' Aunt Ruby nodded at some chick and we nudged past queers with teased hair and studded belts. The doors swung open and music kicked us in the teeth … '*Funky bar full of faces, beautiful faces.*' We pushed and shoved through a crowd of punks and ducked into the loos. Aunt Ruby squatted on her haunches and took out the meth. I kept my eyes peeled, smirking at dumb jokes, graffiti-scribbled walls. She sprinkled the gear in a pipe and sparked a lighter. She clamped her mouth on the barrel and sucked the smoke. Ruby let out a wild grunt. She sprang to her feet, rushing hard. She handed the pipe over and I slugged the dope. We closed our eyes and the hunger subsided—just for a while.

The bar was full of queers, the stench of grog and perfume. Dark lashes thick with make-up peered from shadows—boys laughing, talking tough, girls strutting, striking a pose. Wall-to-wall mirrors reflected blue and red strobes. A hundred eyes were on us but we shrugged them off, stepping through fog to claim our spot on the dance floor. Ruby and I lost ourselves in growling guitars and grinding beats. We hit that floor with a gang of freaks—an angry stampede. Hours disappeared, one song merged into another. Ruby and I thrashed it out till we had nothing left to give. We stomped off the dance floor, hearts racing, catching our breaths. It was hot and damp, everyone circling, closing in. People stared at Ruby's wild hair and thumping strides but she didn't blink. She thumbed her nose at them and punched the door open.

We shoved past thugs trying to drag us into strip clubs, rednecks staggering out of pubs, homeless guys scrounging in gutters. Everyone was out for something but we were on top of the world. Ruby and I fled under the cover of darkness, Iggy Pop ringing in our ears. '*We'll ride through the city tonight … we'll see the city's ripped backsides.*' Oxford Street was dead aside from sweepers churning up and down. Rainbow flags hung sad and limp—all signs of life sucked out of the 'golden mile.' We left it behind, flying high under a canopy of plane trees. Ruby and I weaved over the road, laughing, sighing, a chilly breeze tickled our necks. We rolled up to her bedsit and raced inside before the sky lit up.

I loved her ravishing drapes, classical lamps and animal furs. I loved the scarlet rug on her vinyl lounge. We kicked our shoes off and cranked the stereo, dancing to a Blondie album. Ruby had the most incredible collection of coats, boots and handbags, a queen-size bed and posters splashed on her walls. We swallowed Valium and sprawled on that bed in each other's arms, drifting to sleep after another weekend pounding streets.

We woke to the clang of church bells in the steeple next door. Tenants were shouting and slamming doors, taking showers, clobbering about. Ruby and I curled up in her feather quilt. Hours drifted, the fog from the Valium lifted and the world morphed into view. I twirled Ruby's hair and stroked her deep olive skin. I scanned the crevices and moles on her body, the scars on her arms. I tried to stir her but she wouldn't budge. She lay buried in pillows, guarding her secrets.

I crashed at her place for days, one freak after another bashing on the door. Some rocked up with a warm smile, a loving embrace. Some marched in shooting off at the mouth. Ruby never let them take her for a ride, never let them push her around. She gave them advice, company, a shake-up or a shot of meth. Everyone got what they needed and left feeling better after a visit to Aunt Ruby. She was always one step ahead, knowing things I couldn't see. She pulled me up when I was kidding myself. Ruby said things I knew deep down, things I couldn't face. She said I was foolish and naïve, I took risks I couldn't handle. She said she'd lost too many friends who wouldn't slow down.

*

I saw Ruby a while back, treading Crown Street on a windy day. She was rugged up in a coat, rubbing her arms for warmth. I called her name and she looked up, tears trickling down her face. She spied me through world-weary eyes and ducked into an alley, pretending she was invisible.

That's the last time I saw Aunt Ruby. I hope she's out there somewhere. I hope she got out of that place.

Jean Taylor
Tramming it

When the alarm didn't go off I seriously considered taking another sickie. Except I'd done that once already this week. There were only so many days off a connie could take without a doctor's certificate and I rather suspected I was over the limit as it was. Not that it would worry me unduly if I was sacked from a tram conductor job. I was hardly making a career choice here. But I was desperate to go overseas and without a job had Buckley's hope of getting the money together.

I glanced at the recalcitrant clock. The tram I was supposed to be on would be leaving the yard in another ten minutes. I threw back the bedclothes. If I rushed I'd make it by the time the tram passed the depot again on the way into the city. The spare would cover for me, that's what they were there for. I might even have time for a quick shower.

*

It made a change to be starting work at a somewhat decent hour, I was thinking, as I stepped onto my very favourite (albeit rapidly becoming extinct) mode of transport, one of the old green W-class trams. Almost worth having my pay docked on the strength of it. Although at the rate I was saving the only travelling I'd be able to afford was what I was doing now. It didn't bear thinking about.

Being peak hour the tram was packed with workers. As I pushed my way through the crowd automatically taking money and dispensing tickets I wished I was somewhere else entirely. On Lesbos, for example. I'd never been but I'd heard all about the nude section where the lesbians hung out and the way the tavernas were strung out along the beach front in the village so you could have dinner watching the sun setting into the Aegean.

I was oblivious to the fact that they were hurtling down St Georges Road. In my mind I was now spread-eagled on the hot sand at Skala Eressou smothered in suntan lotion, the sea shushing a few feet away. And best of all, I was surrounded by dozens of naked lesbians who were plying me with Kalamata olives, fetta cheese, fresh peaches smothered in Greek yoghourt and ice cold retsina.

'I said,' a passenger was practically yelling to get my attention, 'I want a two hour concession. If it's not too much bother,' he added sarcastically.

'No bother at all,' I muttered through clenched teeth, 'Could I see your concession card, please?' I only ever did this if passengers got up my nose, like this one. I bared my teeth at him as I handed him the ticket punched for eight o'clock. It was five to. If he hadn't been such a dickhead I'd have given him the extra hour as I usually did.

He handed me a twenty dollar note. I handed him his change in coins, all $18.90 of it. I moved away satisfied that honour had been maintained. It would take more than that to get the better of me.

*

By the time they were crossing Alexander Parade I'd made it to Paris. I was sitting outside one of the patisseries along the Boulevard Saint-Michel, sipping an aperitif before a late dinner for two, the balmy night air caressing my cheek while a dark-haired woman ran her fingers along the inside of my thigh under the table.

I was so taken by this fantasy that I failed to notice that one of my ex-lovers, the one I wasn't talking to, must have got on as they were trundling down Brunswick Street. It wasn't till I'd pulled the cord to signal everyone was on board at Johnston Street that I realised.

My heart gave a painful lurch and settled into a steady rhythm of panic. *Shit, of all the trams on all the tram lines in Melbourne I had to pick this one.* Not only that, she had another woman in tow. *That'd be right.*

Fortunately, the tram was so full they were quite oblivious to me standing there riveted with shock, one arm in the air, my hand still clutching to the cord. *Pull yourself together*, I told myself. *She means nothing to you anymore. It's all over. You've got your own life to lead and you're much better off without her. Remember that!*

It certainly paid me to remember that I didn't at all miss the dramas, the fights, the emotional blackmail and manipulative tears at three in the morning. I relaxed my hold on the cord and chanced a glance in their direction.

I was so startled I did a double take. *It wasn't possible, was it?* That they were standing there, in full view of a crowded tram full of passengers. *Kissing. As if they had the whole tram to themselves.*

I looked around to see how everyone else was taking it. In typical cool Melbourne fashion, by the looks of it. This was Brunswick Street, after all, what could you expect? All these straight passengers from the outskirts of Preston seemed to have shed their suburban prejudices this morning, bless their stretch pantyhose, to incorporate two women kissing, *kissing mind you*, without so much as batting an eyelid.

I put it down to all those articles in the women's magazines about lipstick lesbians which were slanted, to my way of thinking, to be a turn-on for males or as an interesting experiment for straight women or even worse, as something weirdly newsworthy, like serial killers.

And on my tram into the bargain. *Just my luck.* Ordinarily I wouldn't have minded, of course. *If it was anyone else at all.*

*

When I'd had a chance to recover somewhat, I noticed they were not really pashing on, as such. They were cuddling, certainly. Holding hands even and giving each other little, almost inadvertent kisses as the tram lurched and clattered its way towards Gertrude Street. Nothing to get worked up about really and damned if I was going to let anything get to me this morning. And especially not this particular ex-lover.

I turned abruptly and headed back the other way. *Let them have a free ride for all I cared.* 'Tickets. Move away from the door. Tickets please.'

I accepted money and dispensed the odd ticket in between pulling the cord to keep the tram moving. This run couldn't end soon enough for my liking. I braced myself against the back door as the tram turned into Victoria Parade.

Ireland, that's where I wanted to go, *back to the old country* as my mother used to say, to visit the few members of my family who were still alive, cousins mainly. I'd roam the green hills around Belfast as my ancestors had done, drink Guiness by the bloody pintful and watch the sun go down in Galway Bay, to be sure.

'Excuse me,' someone was saying, *wouldn't you know it!* I focused back to the present, rather surprised to find myself moving down Collins Street rather than a country lane with stone walls either side.

'Just down to King Street, please.'

The woman looked familiar, I thought, as I handed her a short-trip ticket and fifty cents change. Really, my memory for faces was getting worse, if anything. Then again, the other woman seemed not to have recognised me either so maybe she just looked like somebody I knew or had been on telly or something?

I pretended to peer out the window to get another look at her face. The woman twigged and smiled. She had the most beautiful brown eyes, I noticed, blushing in embarrassment as I tentatively smiled back.

Then, because I didn't want to seem rude or pushy, I began making my way back to the other end of the tram quite forgetting why I'd stayed up this end in the first place. *Too late.*

My ex and her new lover were getting ready to get off at Russell Street. It only then occurred to me to wonder if maybe she had a job at long last. She was certainly dressed for it in a suit with the obligatory shoulder pads and carrying a briefcase no less. *Must be some salary she was on to look like that,* I mused, trying not to let envy get the better of her by imagining how much sooner I'd be able to get away if I was earning some kind of a decent salary myself.

At that moment it occurred to me that the woman with the brown eyes was Lou Bennett from Tiddas. I had all their CDs but had only managed to get to see them live a couple of times, so no wonder I'd been a bit vague about who she was. I was so delighted that Lou Bennett was actually on my tram that I almost laughed out loud.

It was then my ex turned as she was stepping off the tram and caught the full impact of my excitement. She seemed puzzled at first and possibly smiled or more likely glared back. It was hard to tell for sure before she was obscured by the other passengers and the moment was gone.

The lights changed, I hurriedly pulled the cord twice and the doors closed as the tram trundled on its way. *Safe again.* Really, one of the more positive aspects of being a connie was that I was on the move all the time and not stuck in one place where I could be got at either by phone or by someone inadvertently dropping in. Not usually, anyway. I took a deep breath. It was inevitable that we'd run into each other at some stage. I'd hoped it would be later when I'd completely recovered rather than sooner, like now, that was all.

I was just pulling the cord to keep the tram moving, not even bothering to check tickets as most people were getting off anyway, when I noticed Lou waiting at the door. If the sight of my ex had made my wish I'd stayed in bed that morning after all, the presence of one of my very favourite singers on my tram more than made up for it. Trying not to stare, I stood with one hand on the cord as Lou stepped off the tram and then rang the bells twice and kept watching till she was out of sight.

*

It was always an easy run out of the city at this hour of the morning. As we were changing ends at Spencer Street my driver muttered, 'Must be the school holidays or something. I've never seen so many passengers as we had this morning.'

'Really?' I hadn't noticed.

'You seemed to cope alright,' he added grudgingly.

I accepted the praise as my due. Sitting down up the back and gazing out the window I allowed the events of the morning to play themselves out in my head. By the time we were crossing Spring Street I was back on Lesbos and sipping ouzo in between being massaged all over my bare body by any number of willing lesbian hands.

Adrienne Kisner
Dear Rachel Maddow

From Chapter 1 of *Dear Rachel Maddow*. The author Adrienne Kisner was inspired to write this book by her work with high school and college students. *Dear Rachel Maddow* has been met with strong support from the US mainstream press including *The Los Angeles Times, The Advocate, Salon* and many others.

Folder: Sent
To: Egrimm@westing.pa.edu
From: Brynnieh0401@gmail.com
Date: September 10
Subject: School Assignment

Dear Rachel Maddow,

I am writing to you because of a school assignment. It's a totally ridiculous reason to be writing, but I don't think you'll actually read it anyway. This kind of thing is so sixth grade. I am a junior in high school and I've been forced to write to a "celebrity hero" by the Applied English teacher. (Hey, Mr. Grimm! How's it hanging, buddy?) I wasn't going to do it, because my ex-girlfriend worships you and, hello, school assignment. But I turned on your show and Mom totally freaked out to see me watching you. Apparently your liberal and leftist views don't sit well with her. Mom spat out the words like she was talking about my dad, so I knew she meant it. That made you my celebrity hero.

You were talking about some guys running for Congress. But then you said one of them was "freaking amazing." I don't think newspeople are supposed to say things like that. And isn't that biased? Newspeople aren't supposed to be biased. I know this because Mr. Grimm made us watch this video about newswriting. Though no one else knows this about me, Rachel Maddow, I have a near photographic memory for stuff people say. Their words just stick in my brain. So I remember what a reporter is supposed to do.

Anyway, thanks for pissing off my mom.

Sincerely,

Brynn Harper

Folder: Inbox
To: Brynnieh0401@gmail.com
From: Egrimm@westing.pa.edu
Date: September 11
Subject: RE: School Assignment

Dear Rachel Maddow,

I am writing to you because of a school assignment.

[begin strikethrough]It's a totally ridiculous reason to be writing, but I don't think you actually read it anyway. This kind of thing is so sixth grade**[end strikethrough]. [Brynn, this is good, honest writing. Can you try to put a positive spin on it?]**

I am a junior in high school and I've been forced asked to write to a "celebrity hero" by the Applied English teacher.

[begin strikethrough](Hey, Mr. Grimm! How's it hanging, buddy?)**[end strikethrough] [I'm doing well, thanks. But you can take this out.]**

[begin strikethrough]I wasn't going to do it, because my ex-girlfriend worships you and, hello, school assignment.**[end strikethrough]**

But I turned on your show and Mom totally freaked out to see me watching you. Apparently your liberal and leftist views still don't sit well with her. Mom spat out the words like she was talking about my dad, so I knew she meant it. That made you my celebrity hero. **[Again, great personal touch. But maybe too intimate for this correspondence?]**

You were talking about some guys running for Congress. But then you said one of them was "freaking amazing." And I don't think newspeople are supposed to say things like that. And isn't that biased? Newspeople aren't supposed to be biased. I know this because Mr. Grimm, my Applied English teacher, made us watch this video about newswriting. Though no one else knows this about me, Rachel Maddow, I have a photographic memory for stuff people say. Their words just stick in my brain. So I remember what a reporter is supposed to do. **[You are right, Brynn! I didn't know that about you. Shouldn't you remember your assignments, then?]**

[begin strikethrough]Anyway, thanks for pissing off my mom.**[end strikethrough] [There is a list of questions I asked you to include. Maybe you could end with that instead.]**

Sincerely,
Brynn Harper

Folder: Sent
To: Egrimm@westing.pa.edu
Cc: Rachel@msnbc.com
From: Brynnieh0401@gmail.com
Date: September 12
Subject: School Assignment Again

Dear Rachel Maddow,

I learned an important lesson about rough drafts. If you really want to send someone a letter, you should just send it. Do not turn it in to your English teacher first. But Mr. Grimm (said English teacher) is the only person I know who doesn't think I'm hopeless, so I am trying this again for his sake. Though I'm sending it to you, too, to avoid further editing.

My name is Brynn Harper and I am sixteen years old. I live with my mother and stepfather in Westing, Pennsylvania. I have a brother, too. Or, I had one, anyway.

I first watched your show a couple of times freshman year because my best friend (well, okay, my girlfriend) loved you, so she kind of dragged me along with her. She's not my girlfriend anymore. And she said she didn't have time to watch television anymore, either, even for you. So she dumped us both. That gives us something in common.

I had a list of questions that I was supposed to ask you, but I got most of the answers online already. Mr. Grimm suggested I think of new ones.

So here you go:

1. When you look at the papers on your desk and circle something, are you really reading from them? Don't you read from a teleprompter? When you go to commercial, you shuffle those papers, too. Seriously, is there anything even written on them?
2. How much does a person have to know to be considered a "wonk"?
3. At least one person laughs in the background while you are talking. Is this on purpose? Who is that?
4. Why don't you run for political office?
5. Is there ever a staff meeting when you think to yourself, "Huh, there really isn't a lot going on in the news today"?
6. How many pairs of shoes do you actually own?

Sincerely,
Brynn Harper

Folder: Sent
To: Rachel@msnbc.com
From: Brynnieh0401@gmail.com
Date: September 14
Subject: Jumping for joy

Dear Rachel Maddow,

I am embarrassed to say that I literally squealed in the library when I got your e-mail. I scared the hell out of one of the librarians. She came over to yell at me, and I just sort of jabbed at the computer screen and jumped up and down in my seat. When she figured out that you had written back to me, she just grinned and gave me a thumbs-up.

I made the mistake of forwarding your e-mail to Mr. Grimm. He said I had to answer back again. I was so disgusted with the idea that a good thing would lead to more work that I complained about it at home.

Mom went nuts. I sort of lied and told her I was assigned to write to you (which, technically, was true). She and my stepdad (aka the Fart Weasel, a name I gave him years ago that stuck in my head because even his whiskers smell like fart) then went on an angry rant about bombast and lies and liberals and blah blah blah. The Fart Weasel said he'd even talk to Mr. Grimm on my behalf, which I knew would never happen, because that would require him to make an actual effort in this life. But their reaction sealed my fate. Obviously I would write back to you.

Your fan,
Brynn Harper

Folder: Inbox
To: Brynnieh0401@gmail.com
From: Egrimm@westing.pa.edu
Date: September 17
Subject: RE: The Blues

Dear Rachel Maddow,

Mr. Grimm has used the fact that you wrote back to me after our hero assignment to discuss "cause and effect."

[begin strikethrough]This might seem pretty basic for a junior English class, but because I gave up on being Brynn the Scholar a while ago, the effect is that I am in the basement of the school, where the rooms don't have numbers, only colors. **[end strikethrough] [Brynn — I don't mind if you retain the epistolary format for assignments, if this is what inspires you to do your work. However, keep in mind that if you intend to send this, you might want to be a little less confessional and a little more formal.]**

Us "Applied" juniors are in the blue room (as opposed to the Honors/AP or Academic students allowed to walk in the sun aboveground). I started freshman year on the Honors track, but was shuffled into Academic shortly into my sophomore year. By the end of it, my mom said I was going to end up like my brother and I had better get my act together. My journalism teacher referred me for a shit ton of assessments, which got me into Applied, where I could get "more attention." I thought all I needed was to give more of a shit, but it turns out speech-to-text technology makes me a writing fiend. (Note: I still actually need to give more of a shit.) We have three teachers who teach us in shifts along with the ninth, tenth, and twelfth graders. They always look tired, even with near constant caffeination. **[Good use of imagery, but let us both agree never to share this with the rest of your faculty.]**

Passing junior and senior year in the Applied Color Room Kingdom is Brynnie's Last Chance at graduating, because the numbered rooms of tiny Westing High gave up on the Brynnster for good last May.

The blue room crew is cool. The best of us is Lacey, who chills in her wheelchair using her voice board to communicate. She is quick with that thing, and her brain works about a thousand times faster than mine. She is actually an Honors/AP senior, though I don't hold that against her. Since she's the smartest person ever, the school lets her do basically whatever she wants. She gets bored with high school classes and even the extra community college classes she takes. Thus she spends a lot of time with us as a 'resident peer tutor'. This works out for me because she's super-nice and has kind of taken me on as a special project. Greg, Lance, Riley, Bianca, and I (the Applied junior crew) basically see Lacey as another teacher.

Do you get lost effects from lost causes? I'll have to ask Mr. Grimm. I think he'd be happy to learn I was paying attention to the lesson. **[You know … I actually am. Though none of you are lost causes. Please consider adding a few more paragraphs addressing the specifics of this assignment, "Cause and Effect in My Daily Life."]**

Sincerely,

Brynn

Folder: Drafts
To: Rachel@msnbc.com
From: Brynnieh0401@gmail.com
Date: September 18
Subject: Got the blues

Dear Rachel Maddow,

I had a pen pal once in fifth grade. I loved writing to her, even if I hated the physical act of writing. It felt good to put all my words some place. So, I'll keep writing to you. Don't tell Mr. Grimm. If he knew I was doing it so much on my own, it might go to his head.

Today, to suck as much as humanly possible out of something interesting, Mr. Grimm put us in pairs to talk about our hero assignments. Peer Mentor Lacey was stuck with me. She did the assignment just for fun even though she didn't have to.

"So, that's the lady with the one eyebrow?" I said of her hero.

"Yes." Lacey sighed. She did that a lot with me. "But she painted herself as she was, see…."

"But she's dead. You wrote to a dead person?"

"I interpreted the assignment. She is famous. She is my hero. Like Grimm would argue with me. I'm not even a student in this class."

"Well played." I whistled. I was mostly annoyed that I didn't think of something like that.

"And you like a pundit. Fascinating."

"She is a scholar and a storyteller," I said, bowing my head reverently and putting my hand on my heart. "Politics are her canvas."

Lacey chuckled. "Well. We both like artists, then."

"Yes."

"Did you know that Frida Kahlo was also in a wheelchair?" Lacey said.

"No. I don't think I did. Did you know that Rachel was the first out Rhodes Scholar?"

"Yes."

"Of course you did," I said. "You know everything."

"Not everything."

"Seems like it." I crossed my arms. "Are you sure you don't want to go out with me?"

"I had to agree not to date my mentees. You and I have had this discussion. Also, I'm still into guys."

"Fine. That makes no sense to me. But fine."

Lacey laughed. Her laugh sounds a little like wind chimes.

Sincerely,

Brynn

Visit bentstreet.net for our *Bent Street 2* contributor bios

https://bentstreet.net/bent-street-2-contributors/

Bent Street welcomes contributions – from Australia and overseas – at any time and publishes material ongoing in the Bent Street Café.

bentstreet.net

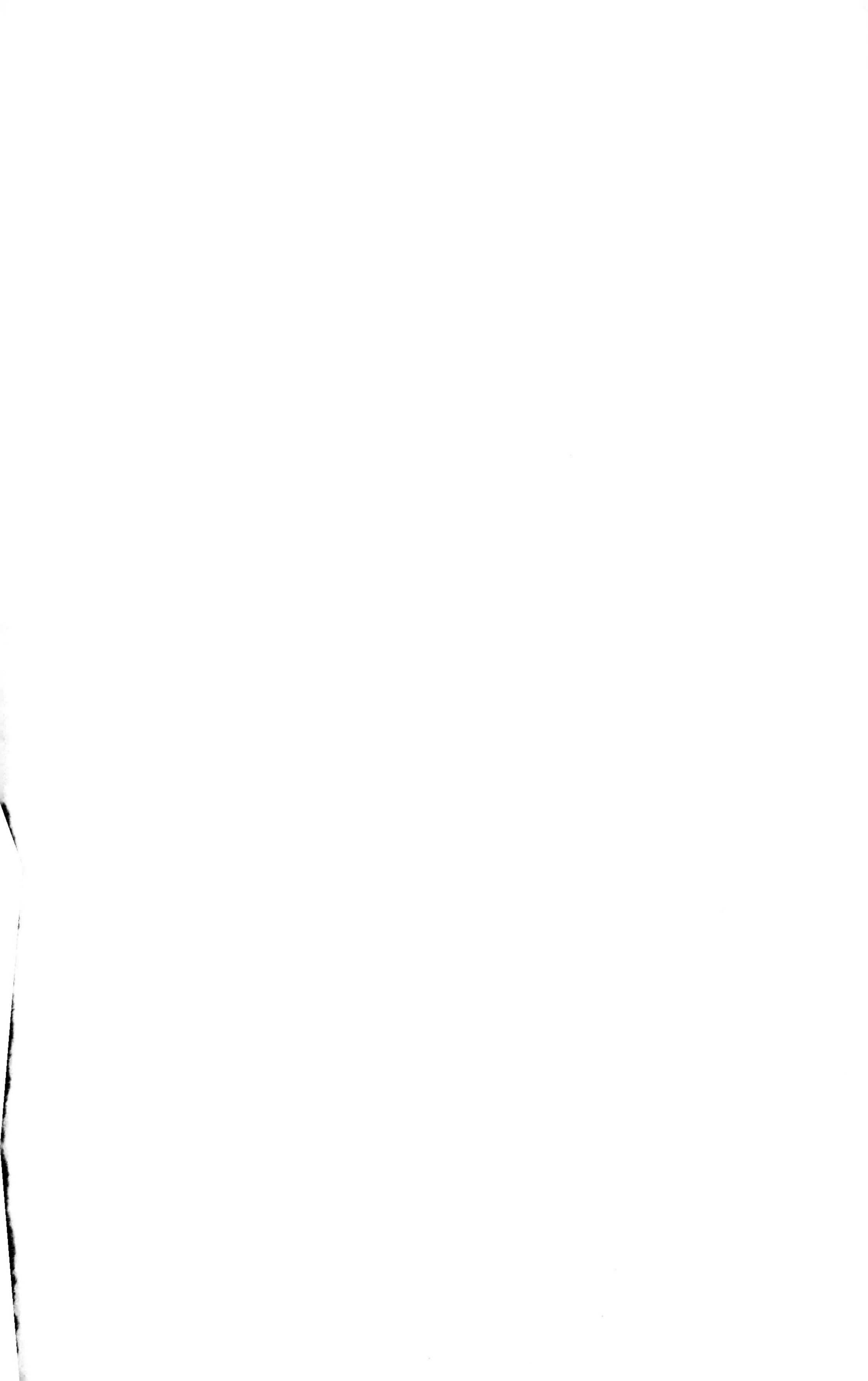

www.ingramcontent.com/pod-product-compliance
Lightning Source LLC
LaVergne TN
LVHW052351100826
845147LV00013B/816

* 9 7 8 0 6 4 8 4 6 0 4 0 4 *